Summoning the Ghosts

TALES OF MICHIGAN CENTRAL STATION

JERRY CONNOR

MINDSTIR MEDIA

Published by Mindstir Media, LLC
45 Lafayette Rd | Suite 181| North Hampton, NH 03862 | USA
1.800.767.0531 | www.mindstirmedia.com

Printed in the United States of America
ISBN: 978-1-958729-44-1

This is a work of fiction. Many of the events and characters inspiring these tales were reported contemporaneously in the Detroit Free Press. These are still available in the newspapers archives and are an invaluable source of history as it was originally recorded. Some events and characters are entirely fictional based on the events of the period. These were intended to be illustrative of an era in Detroit history encompassing much of the 20th century. Wars, riots, a changing economic climate, political upheaval, and the struggles of the civil rights movement are the background for these stories. Every effort was made to re-create these tumultuous times accurately. Taken as a whole, these tales are a window to our past, as well as a sign post towards our future.

Contents

Whistle Stop 1

SEPTEMBER 2020

The Project

Like many fellow Detroiters, I found myself in a long queue on a hot stormy Saturday afternoon hoping for a chance to visit the abandoned Michigan Central railroad station. It is situated on Michigan Avenue at the edge of Corktown. That historic Detroit neighborhood has in recent years become an epicenter for legions of young urban homesteaders; purchasing and restoring the vintage buildings, and contributing to a cultural revitalization of the entire district. Until now that booming environment has not included the station itself. It has remained aloof from all the excitement surrounding it; sullenly brooding over its isolation. But all of this is about to change. In 2018, the property was purchased by the Ford Motor Company as part of an ambitious vision to build a tech center in the heart of the city. To stimulate interest and excitement for the project, Ford executives offered the public a chance to view the property before the renovations began. Entrance was limited to those who pre-enrolled and interest was far greater than expected. Those without reservations took their chances standing in line, hoping for eventual walk up admission. After decades of abandonment and neglect the venerable old edifice is in sad disrepair. Those standing in queue had plenty of time to view the wreckage years of desertion has inflicted on the once proud structure. Despite its shabby appearance, unmistakable vibrations of renewal were pulsing over the property. The long line of people snaked around the switch back chutes contributed to the excited buzz. On this particular day, my patience would be frustrated by a midafternoon downpour thwarting my chance to actually get in. I will have to wait to see the finished result in the coming years.

In the last 40 years this historic property has come to symbolize the plight of Detroit. The diminished use and eventual abandonment of the station reflected the decline of the city from which it rose. The prosperity and economic clout of Detroit has ebbed during the last century, as the global automotive industry has evolved. The status of the city as indisputable center of the auto world is now being shared with focal points in Europe and Asia. To keep pace with this global competition the domestic manufacturers had to find ways to become more efficient. This necessitated employing fewer workers and many lower skilled workers lost their jobs. Growing unemployment resulted in a shrinking tax base which eroded municipal services causing a mass exodus out of the city. Accelerating the decline has been the intractability of racial inequality. One hundred fifty years after the Civil War we are still riven by the failure to live up to our ideal "All men are created equal". Perhaps the restoration of the old station is a step in the right direction towards economic renewal and social justice.

I greatly appreciated my time in the shadow of the great building. I sensed the energy of all the politicians, artists, industrialists, athletes, criminals and commuters who had come this way for purposes unique to their life stories. I could almost hear the tramping of countless spectral footfalls. An idea gradually took form. Why not give voice to some of the stories of the people and events whose ghosts haunt this ancient space? This seems, like the restoration itself, a worthy project.

Standing before this great terminal calls to mind the colorful pageant of the past witnessed by these silent walls. The rise and fall and the rebirth of the railroad station is synonymous with the city itself, an indispensable chapter of the greater American saga. Millions of passengers over the decades blended their comings and goings into a single narrative. It is Detroit's Ellis Island, where multitudes of restive but hopeful people met at the intersection of circumstance and aspiration. All people are passengers through this world and our combined journeys weave the epic tapestry of history. Most of our lives are concealed by obscurity, but all human beings have unique stories to tell. In the end we all leave our footprints on the shifting sands of time.

Whistle Stop 2

NEW YEAR'S EVE 1933

The Fugitive

The great clock over the ticket counter adjoining the main waiting room read 11:25 PM. Just over 30 minutes to the New Year. The cavernous space of the Michigan Central Station was surprisingly crowded at this late hour. A few trains were still scheduled for arrival and departure in the overnight hours. Expectant passengers waited in small knots, some trying to stretch out on uncomfortable mahogany benches, others passing brown paper bags among them with no real effort to disguise their contents. Many ragged people skulked in the shadows trying to look as if they had a reason to be there beyond escaping the bitter cold outside. The restaurant was disgorging its remaining celebrants, many of whom staggered unsteadily towards the exit leading to Roosevelt Park and Michigan Avenue beyond. Those partyers remaining in the dining rooms awaited the arrival of midnight to pop the corks on chilled champagne bottles and raise a toast to better days. There was an unmistakable buzz in the air, a melody of restless music: people in motion and the solemnity of the moment when an old year dies. Hopeful, sentimental, determined, melancholy, such was the mood among the assembled pilgrims in Michigan Central Station awaiting the arrival of 1934.

This moment in time occurred simultaneously in two epochal chapters of American history, one drawing to a close and another showing no signs of let up. By 1933 it was obvious to all that Prohibition did not work and could not continue. Far from preventing social ills, violence among rival bootleggers made things much worse. Through it all, people continued to drink and there was no real way to stop it. Ultimately the government bowed to the obvious and succumbed to the desire for a piece of the action. Prohibition was repealed on December 5, 1933 when the 21st amendment to the constitution went into effect just in time for the crowd in Michigan Central station to enjoy a long denied legal holiday bender.

The beginning and end of Prohibition overlapped the collapse of the global economy signaled by the stock market crash of 1929. During this period, people had to endure the misery of hard times without the palliative of drink. The Great Depression hit Detroit industries hard. Idle assembly lines put people out of work. And since the unemployed had no income to purchase goods and services produced by other workers, the whole destructive cycle accelerated. The city wore the scowling face of hard times. Even the annual Hudson parade just a month before was a subdued affair and failed to lift the municipal spirit to its accustomed holiday gaiety. Turning the corner toward prosperity was more than a decade away.

At this point we note the arrival on the scene of a nondescript man dressed in a cheap brown suit. He was dressed like a traveler, economy class with a leather valise and a railway ticket out of town protruding from his overcoat breast pocket. His destination Saint Louis, departure 12:45 AM. He thoroughly scans the scattered groups of people as if he is looking for someone. The man pauses to check the time then settles onto a bench maintaining his watchfulness. He is 32 years old. In the semi darkness he begins to take stock in his future. Mentally he surveys his assets. It is a relatively short list. His comparative youth and the $10,000 he carries in his valise are all he has to bring to his new start somewhere far from his Detroit home. Forces beyond his control or understanding have forced him into an early retirement. But if he can manage to avoid the long reach of the Purple Gang, from whom he stole the money, he might have a chance to start over. His name was Patrick Keillor and he was a retired bootlegger on the run.

Keillor was born and raised in nearby Corktown, in a poor working class Irish household. His father, a hard drinking abusive man, abandoned his wife and child and was never around much in Patrick's childhood. His mother Mona was a devout and hardworking woman who made sure her rowdy only child, no matter his misbehavior during the week, was in the pew at Most Holy Trinity Parish Sunday morning.

Keillor's mother's extended family and acquaintances included a wide cross section of the Corktown community. Everyone from the Grand Knight of the Knights of Columbus, to the cop on the beat and the ward alderman had at one time or another taken coffee at Mona Keillor's kitchen table. So it was that young Patrick grew up with a wide circle of friends and a network of social contacts that would prove useful. But his most fateful relationship would be with his cousin Sean Clancy, his boyhood friend and idol, whose influence would shape the rest of his life. Sean was the brother Patrick never had. The Clancys and Keillors were neighbors. The two boys spent many carefree summer afternoons playing stickball in the streets, innocently plotting their next adventure. Over time the boys grew into the hyper-aggressive, dog-eat-dog society characteristic of hard times, Side by side they reached unruly manhood. All of this Mona watched with patient apprehension.

The loose group of street toughs that would become the notorious Purple Gang was already active long before Prohibition began. They started out as rowdy youngsters and petty thieves. They dipped their toe into the pool of criminality by swiping cigarettes, snatch and grab; which could be smoked or easily sold for a quick buck. They were the schoolyard bullies and juvenile delinquents who rampaged the neighborhood and generally made trouble for anyone vulnerable to intimidation. As time passed they graduated to illegal activity requiring more muscle, armed robbery and extortion. But the onset of Prohibition in 1929 was the golden opportunity that propelled them to full-fledged criminal enterprise.

Sean Clancy was among the smartest and most ruthless of the Irish ruffians who ruled Corktown. He foresaw quickly what the market place demanded. He shrewdly went about building a network of thirsty speakeasies that he supplied with liquor. At his side, Patrick was a junior partner limited to simple, less dangerous activity. Errands mostly; chauffeuring passengers, occasionally the more dangerous transport of liquor, guns, or money. This narrow role in the business was partly due to Sean's desire to keep his cousin safe. Beyond Clancy's concerns for Patrick's welfare, he harbored reservations about his cousin's suitability for this kind of work. Patrick, was dependable as a courier but a little soft hearted, too forgiving of grudges, too slow to press any advantage, not quite ruthless enough. Clancy had none of these limitations and the two managed quite well, joined as they were in mutual trust. Patrick was content despite his low rank. Business was booming and he, like all his criminal colleagues, couldn't help but prosper. He was bringing home $125 a week, a staggering sum for the times. He bought Mona a new house on a shady street in Corktown and a new 1932 Ford Model B which remained parked on the street since she was terrified of learning to drive it. She was, for her part, suspicious of all this sudden wealth. But times being hard and her devotion to her son absolute, she was willing to accept his stories of big business deals he and Clancy had pulled off. She dared not question further. In the deep recesses of her heart she was afraid for her son and prayed for him daily.

Detroit was ideally situated to become the behemoth of the bootlegging business. Canada with its industrial complex of distilleries and breweries was barely a mile away across the river. Toronto and Windsor boomed as liquor production expanded to satisfy the American market. Transport to the United States was straight forward enough but hazardous, across the swift flowing Detroit River. The ships that carried this illegal cargo avoided detection from American customs inspectors by carrying manifests for delivery of cargo from Canada to Cuba or Central America. Secretly they would off load their illegal cargo to warehouses on the American side of the river. Countless boats of all sizes made the round trip of pickup and delivery in the warmer months. If the river froze over in winter and the ice was safely solid, toboggans and sometime passenger cars crossed the ice to deliver shipments to rival distributors who battled each other for shares of the illicit trade. Law enforcement and local governments tried to interdict the illegal traffic but could never quite manage to staunch the flow. The demand was simply too great and the profits too rich to stop it. And so, despite the government's inconsistent efforts, the lucrative trade continued. The future seemed bright for the growing Detroit underworld.

As time went by Clancy saw the enormous potential of the interstate business. Cities like Chicago and Indianapolis were much further from Canadian supply but just as thirsty as Detroit. Gradually the focus shifted from servicing the Detroit market to developing a far reaching distribution network into new markets as far away as Kansas City and Atlanta. The business model was evolving. Selling liquor in Detroit speakeasies was less important to the syndicate then interstate distribution. This required the involvement of the powerful Teamsters union and numerous local police and government agencies, all skimming the fat from the business. No matter how thinly the pie was sliced, the rewards were considerable for everyone. More and more the Detroit business was turned over to trusted confederates living in the city. Opportunity had come knocking on Patrick Keillor's door. He assumed exclusive control of three speakeasies, one in Corktown and two off Gratiot Avenue near the eastern market. For the most part the local cops were on the take and compliant with his business interests. Patrick was insulated from much of the violence of rival factions. Life was good and business continued to grow.

But political winds were already gathering that would blow away this way of life like the sands of the Oklahoma Dust Bowl. By 1932 the nations tolerance of Prohibition had soured and now it was evident it could not last much longer. When Prohibition was over, the speakeasies upon which the bootleggers depended would all disappear overnight like dinosaurs after the comet.

Clancy as usual, saw this first. Never one to go down without a fight he launched a simple but profitable scheme to steal as much as he could before the business went under for good. Assisted by accomplices in several cooperative speakeasies he would deliver short shipments of liquor but be paid for full ones. This undelivered merchandize would then be sold again to double the conspirator's profits. One of his accomplices was his cousin Patrick. The plan worked very well and the two cousins were soon pocketing healthy profits. Clancy took a step too far and that would prove his undoing. Driven by greed and the overconfidence of his own cleverness, Clancy launched a highjacking of a rival's shipment bound for transport down south. Five of the rival bootleggers were gunned down in the resulting battle. Nickel and dime larceny could be concealed by creative bookkeeping but violence and theft against a rival bootlegger could not be ignored. Three days after Christmas, the body of his cousin Clancy, obviously fingered by the mob, was found bullet riddled in a seedy back alley in Ypsilanti. Patrick concluded it was a favorable time to skip town. His escape plan, carefully planned in advance, was dangerous but staying in Detroit was certain death. His chances depended on an elaborate misdirection, arranged by Clancy that ought to open a brief window for his escape. In the end everything depended on Clancy's silence before he was killed. If he had given Patrick up, then he was doomed and escape was impossible. But either way he had to try and make a run for it; which explains his presence in the Michigan Central Station on a frigid New Year's Eve clutching a bag of the mob's money, waiting for a late night train out of town.

He thought of many things as the minutes ticked relentlessly toward midnight. He thought of Mona and schemed how he might eventually get word to her. He also wanted to make sure as much of his loot as possible could find its way to ease her old age. It wounded him to think of her pain and bewilderment when she realized he had left without saying goodbye, but he dared not take the chance. He thought of Clancy and all his boyhood friends and the only home he had ever known, all left behind. But the one overriding concern he had was how long he could avoid the vengeance he was certain was being planned for him. He wondered how long he could stay alive.

These sobering thoughts were interrupted by the approach of a small ragged looking boy he had not noticed before. Patrick was instantly alert to the threat and his hand moved instinctively to his jacket pocket. Behind him was a woeful looking young woman, hardly more than a girl. Both looked terrified to approach him but too desperate not to try. Patrick relaxed, sensing no danger. The girl began in a small plaintive voice to tell her story. Her words blurred; mere notes in a hymn of misery. "Out on the street; frightened; hungry; cold; for the love of God, Mister, please help, help, help". Patrick listened impassively as she finished her heartbreaking tale and broke down in uncontrollable sobs. Patrick reached into his pocket and produced a handkerchief which he handed to the girl. He then turned his attention to the boy. The child's mild, hopeful expression suggested he was kind hearted and soft spoken; and Patrick could not escape the feeling he had seen him somewhere before. Maybe it was a glimpse of his former self, or the pain of leaving home, or the thought of his beloved mother, or the Great Clock counting down the arrival of the New Year; or the feeling of solidarity with others in jeopardy that moved him to open the bag and carefully extract a short stack of bills. He passed them into her astonished grasp, stood up and said simply: "Happy New Year". He turned without another word and moved toward his platform. "What the hell," he told himself; "It was dirty money anyway."

At 12:55 AM on New Year's Day the late train to Saint Louis left the Michigan Central Station with Patrick Keillor slumped in his seat. He breathed a sigh of relief and mouthed a silent prayer of thanksgiving to his cousin Clancy who had kept his secret. Patrick raised a glass in a silent toast to his cousin's memory. Through the window of his coach, the familiar surroundings of his hometown dissolved into mist. The train, beginning his pilgrimage to redemption, gathered speed as it raced through the countryside with the hopes and dreams of all onboard rushing towards a dark night and a new morning. Patrick closed his eyes and fell into a dreamless sleep.

Whistle Stop 3

NEW YEAR'S EVE 1933

The Children

The young woman was thunderstruck as she stared into the semi darkness at the retreating man moving toward the departure platforms. The boy, her younger brother, huddled close to her side uncomprehending. The girl, during her desperate plea to the mysterious stranger, had been sobbing in anguish. The tears continued to roll down her cheeks but now her expression reflected relief and bewildered joy. For no reason she could understand, this man, possibly some heavenly emissary, had handed her an unbelievable gift, an enormous sum of money. She was immediately sensible of her vulnerable position standing in open view in the waiting room of Michigan Central. She grabbed her brother Larry's, hand and deliberately, so as not to attract attention, retreated into the dark recesses of an empty alcove. Once there, turning her back to any prying eyes she carefully examined the bundle she clutched in her trembling hands. Ten one hundred dollar bills. (In today's dollars roughly $15,000) A fortune. Her disbelief turned to terror when she realized that people would kill for such a sum. She knew instinctively this money could not be honest and dangerous people would be searching for it. Her first impulse was to throw the money away and escape. But how? She tucked the bills into her purse. This gift was their salvation but also put them in terrible jeopardy. She and her brother were all alone without protection in a city that had turned against them. The grip of hard times had nearly everyone by the throat. Robbery and murder were a predictable fate for anyone who carelessly displayed their wealth.

Despite her youth, (she turned 19 the week before Christmas) Evelyn Donnelly was mature and competent. She had been looking after Larry for the six months since her father, Chance, had died in a freak industrial accident, an ironic victim of his own name. Her mother, Alice, had died of cancer shortly after 11 year old Larry was born. Sister and brother were alone in a world without a safety net and no nearby family to help.

Evelyn had held a steady job since before her father died. She was a cashier and tellers assistant at a branch bank of Wells Fargo on Woodward Avenue. She seemed to have a knack for the banking business and instinctive understanding of the mysteries of money management. Bright and ambitious, she had looked after her father and brother, held down her job, and attended Business College at night where she studied shorthand, typing, and bookkeeping. All that changed when her father died. The demands of adult responsibility overwhelmed her. Her job performance deteriorated with her morale and she was let go from the bank. She was reduced to cleaning houses and occasional babysitting jobs. Sister and brother lived in a small flat but could hardly make ends meet. When their situation attracted the notice of the city's truancy officers, their situation worsened.

They were deemed to be vagrants, and Larry because of his age, declared a ward of the city. Evelyn learned to her horror that her brother was to be delivered to the custody of the city orphanage. Evelyn took Larry and fled. For three terrifying and miserable days they lived on the street, trying to stay alive. Finally, near the end of their rope, hungry and freezing, they found themselves loitering in front of Michigan Central on a bitter cold New Year's Eve. Not knowing what else to do, they fearfully entered. If they could just warm themselves for a while…

The more Evelyn thought about the problem of this burdensome wealth the less certain she was how to proceed. She needed money desperately, they were starving, but all this money could not buy them a cup of coffee. She knew instinctively producing a $100 bill would instantly raise suspicion, especially from a young woman. She couldn't spend it without risking dangerous attention. She knew it would be fool hardy to try to change one of the bills to smaller, less suspicious, denominations. Hundred dollar bank notes were so rare and noticeable in circulation that they became almost useless for her purposes. She needed to make a sufficiently large purchase with one of the bills that produced a small amount of change; then they could at least get something to eat. But what could she possibly buy that was expensive enough but would not attract attention? Even if she figured that out, there was still the problem of what to do with the remaining cash. It was clear as long she was in possession of any of it she and Larry would be in danger. Gradually, she worked out a desperate plan to solve both problems but it would have to wait until morning when the ticket office opened. In the meantime they went hungry while she held in her purse the means to feast at the finest restaurant in the city. She and Larry spent a restless night trying to avoid the notice of the station's security officers. The dawn was slow in coming. More than once she dozed off and drifted into a fevered dream of armed men chasing her down an empty street with bullets whizzing close to her head.

When the ticket office opened at 9:30 AM the first customer in line was a young girl hand-in-hand with an even younger boy.

"Please sir. How much is the fare for two one way tickets to San Francisco?"

She chose that location because it was certainly far enough away to be an expensive ticket. She had also heard it was pretty, and that settled the matter. Because of her banking experience, she knew there was a Western Union office there. That was a necessary part of her plan.

The clerk without looking up asked perfunctorily:

"Two adults"?

When he glanced up and saw Evelyn he asked, more curious than suspicious:

"Miss, how old are you?"

"Twenty two" Evelyn lied. "And my brother is 14". Another lie.

The clerk scribbled a few calculations on a note pad.

"$32.50 each for coach. He added as if it was unnecessary: "$45.50 for first class. First class includes complimentary meals in the club car." (in today's dollars first class transport for the two of them was nearly $1400)

Evelyn did the math in her head. Perfect. Although she had not been asked by the ticket agent she volunteered her prepared cover story. She hoped it sounded convincing. Uncle living in California. Christmas gift. Going for visit. Wired money.

The clerk seemed disinterested with her story until Evelyn concluded:

"Two First class tickets, please."

"That will be 91.00 dollars" he said rather dubiously, regarding her shabby appearance.

Evelyn produced a carefully crumpled C note and laid it on the counter. She had purposely tried to masquerade the bills crispness by wadding it up and smudging it. Her ruse worked. The bill had the appearance of having been circulated. The clerk was impressed. He produced the two ticket coupons and handed them over.

"Have a nice trip. I hope it's a lot warmer there than here. Train this morning leaves at 11:40 AM from platform 12. On the California Zephyr. Happy New Year".

Evelyn pocketed her $9 change. She and Larry immediately made their way to an open breakfast counter and feasted on toast and scrambled eggs, their first real meal in three days. Feeling much better Evelyn rehearsed her next move. All that remained before departure was to visit the Western Union office on the other side of the station.

Another carefully prepared cover story:

"Please Sir. I am attending college in California. I would like to wire the money for my tuition and expenses to the Western Union office in San Francisco so I can pick it up there. I really don't want to carry cash."

"Very sensible" the clerk replied. "How much will you be wiring?"

"875 dollars" Evelyn replied. (Over $13,000 in today's value). She decided to keep some cash with her for expenses on arrival in San Francisco. Twenty five dollars should do nicely.

Again, the clerk seemed impressed but also slightly disconcerted. For a moment he hesitated. This seemed an unusual transaction and he really ought to consult his boss. But the practical concern of awakening his notoriously bad tempered boss so early on New Year's Day squelched that impulse. Over time the government would regulate wired funds and establish strict procedures to provide greater security to the process. On this particular morning Evelyn benefitted from an annoyed clerk who really did not want to be there so early this holiday morning. Despite his misgivings, he quickly produced the paperwork and completed the transaction. He added without enthusiasm or sincerity "Have a nice trip"

The California Zephyr departed Detroit carrying a train load of passengers settling in for the long 3 day cross country trip. Among their number were lawyers and engineers, all affluent and prominent, bound on journeys momentous and mundane. Included among them were two small but hopeful refugees bound on a journey as consequential as any on board. Evelyn remembered her father telling her of an army buddy he had met in France when they both served as doughboys in General Pershing's army. He had gone on to success in the burgeoning motion picture industry in his native southern California after discharge. The two men had been close friends and comrades in war time. They vowed to remain close and pledged a reunion at earliest opportunity. Evelyn resolved to try and find her father's friend. Perhaps he could help?

At nearly the same hour, in Saint Louis Union station, Patrick Keillor was arriving on the platform. He thought briefly of the poor children he had encountered back in Detroit. Wondered what became of them. Wished them well. But more practical and immediate concerns intervened. What happens now? He dismissed the thought of the vagrant children and began to walk purposefully toward the exit.

Whistle Stop 4

SEPTEMBER 30, 1945

The Reunion

P atrick Keillor had lived as a fugitive in East St Louis Illinois for over a decade. He was successful in escaping discovery by the mob and managed to live in safe yet uneasy anonymity. In time Patrick made the transition from being a marked man to being a forgotten one. Each passing year, more and more of his criminal colleagues from the old days were either dead or in jail. Those few that were still around were trying to live quietly in retirement, hoping that their past would not catch up and betray them. Patrick's vigilance relaxed but never ceased. He had enough recollection of his cousin Clancy's fate to remind him to stay alert. Even though most of the founding king-pins of the Purple Gang were gone or elderly, the criminal enterprise they spawned had stretched its tentacles to every big city in the country, including St, Louis. They were a new generation of criminals, less conspicuous, but every bit as dangerous as their fathers. It was the war rather than the cops that had intervened to keep them relatively quiet. But a vendetta, even an old one, would never expire without being avenged.

Patrick's biggest fear when he left Detroit in 1933 was that the mob would threaten his mother, Mona, to try and get to him. Patrick still had money and a network of loyal friends from the old days in Detroit. He arranged protection for Mona in his absence. In August 1935, the *Detroit Free Press* printed a story of a gun battle near Corktown between the police and a number of gangsters. Two of the mobsters were killed. The violence had occurred only several blocks removed from Mona Keillor's neighborhood. The paper was not certain the cause of the violence and speculated it was another example of turf warfare between rival gangs. Far away, Patrick knew better. His insurance policy was working. The Mob made no second attempt. Mona, for the present, was safe.

Patrick prospered but never ostentatiously. He had married and in time a son and daughter completed his family. He appeared to the entire world as a comfortable middle- aged family man living a pleasant life. Not even a hint of his past remained. By shrewd investments he was financially secure. He was a silent partner in an automotive dealership and a construction contracting business from which he drew a respectable income. He continued to pay a sizeable amount to maintain protection of Mona, but was glad to do so. He continued to make anonymous deposits to her bank accounts so that now in her old age every need was provided. So far he had avoided direct contact with her just to be on the safe side. But Patrick knew Mona had one unfulfilled need. He knew she desperately desired to see her son and grandchildren before she died. The thought of his elderly mother living alone, even in the comfort and security he provided, tormented him. Patrick decided to risk a visit. Certainly enough time had passed and he would be safe? But then he thought of Clancy. Ever cautious, he would make the trip by himself not wishing to put his family at risk. The ecstatic confusion of the end of the war should give him cover. If all went well, a larger family reunion would soon follow.

Patrick discussed with his wife his travel plans and they reached an agreement. He consulted a calendar and carefully evaluated potential scheduling conflicts. Finally he found a workable date. He picked up the telephone and called the railway ticket office: One round trip fare to Michigan Central departing September 30. He notified the intermediary he used to contact Mona to let her know he was coming. He placed letters from his children to their grandmother as well recent photos in a large envelope and placed it in his brown leather valise. Patrick, after twelve long years of sojourning following his desperate escape, was completing the journey in reverse. He was going home.

Bill Waverly was a large genial man with an expansive manner and a winning smile. It was 1935 and he lived in a comfortable house in the Hollywood Hills with his 20-year- old son, Rex. A veteran of the First World War, Bill had returned to his native California to pursue a career in the motion picture industry. He had built a solid reputation as a movie producer and sometimes director. He was said to have the golden touch. The projects he chose to work on usually got made, and more importantly made money. His wife and he had divorced some years back when she left him for a casting director promising a role in a film that was never made. That was Hollywood for you.

Rex, Bill's son, stood a towering six foot five inches, so naturally his friends dubbed him "Shorty". He was a ball player and a good one. A rangy left hander with a blazing fastball and a wicked curve, he terrorized the semi pro leagues. On a barnstorming trip to northern California he dominated the local lineup of a good Bay Area team. His performance was witnessed by the future Yankee Hall of Famer Tony Lazzeri who was a California resident and was present at the game. Lazzeri was very impressed with the hard throwing youngster. He passed the word and in time scouts from all around the American League came calling. Shorty Waverly seemed on his way to the Big Leagues.

Today Bill was in his study re-reading a telegram he had received from the daughter of his old army buddy, Chance Donnelly. His memory strayed back many years ago to 1917. Assigned to the same regiment in France the two had been best friends. Chance had saved his life when he had been knocked cold by the concussion of an exploding shell. He had fallen dazed and bleeding into a shell crater. In the confusion, he was left behind when his unit fell back. It was Chance who risked his own life to return to the battlefield to find his friend and carry him back to the safety of the American trenches. Bill had learned of Chance's passing in Detroit two years ago and quietly grieved for his friend. Now unexpectedly, was a telegram from Chance's daughter. The message was brief. She had moved to San Francisco from Detroit last year with her brother Larry. Would love to meet. Of course, Bill had wired back immediately. The date had been quickly arranged. Now a week later, the reunion was to take place the next day. Bill and Shorty would drive to Los Angeles tomorrow in the Packard and pick up their visitors at the railway station.

Evelyn Donnelly had never looked back from her desperate escape from Detroit just ahead of the mob's retribution. The money she had wired ahead was deposited in the local bank and was completely undetectable to anyone who might still be looking for it. Every so often she allowed herself a moment of self-satisfaction. She had pulled it off. She had gotten away cleanly. After struggling in Detroit, California seemed like paradise. The milder climate was wonderful. She had found a job quickly in a bank and was doing well. Larry attended a nearby school and had proven a brilliant student. Best of all, they had purchased a small house with a view of the bay. It seemed a perfect time to visit her father's friend Bill Waverly. She had left Detroit hoping he might be a benefactor. Now that she no longer needed his assistance, she was hoping to acquire his friendship.

The Waverlys were waiting on the platform when the train from San Francisco arrived. They spotted their guests the instant they stepped off the train. Bill fairly gasped when he spotted Larry. The youngster was a dead ringer for his father, as a younger man. The same features, the same self-assured gaze; everything. Bill rejoiced to see Chance's face again even as a copy. Bill enfolded Evelyn in a welcoming embrace: "Your father would be so proud of you both" He turned to introduce Shorty and this time it was Evelyn who fairly gasped. He was the most handsome man she had ever seen. Tall, lean, with even features and short cropped blond hair, she nervously stammered her hello. For Shorty's part he found this young woman pretty and fascinating. He was instantly intrigued by her obvious competence and maturity. The other girls he knew tended to be giggly and flirtatious. This one was definitely different.

Life took its predictable course. In good times and in bad, for reasons only the heart can explain, two young people meet and fall in love. So it was with Shorty and Evelyn, but it would not be easy. He traveled frequently on barnstorming trips through the region while she continued to live in the Bay Area. They saw each other as frequently as they could but they both became accustomed to separations. Their wedding day would have to wait until some permanent solution could be found. They depended on the old saying; "Love will find a way". The "way" love found for them was totally unexpected and one of the great ironies of Evelyn's life. In 1937 Shorty got a call from the Detroit Tigers. The team was looking to fill a hole in their rotation with a southpaw and offered him a job. Finally they could be married. The town she had fled so desperately three years ago was calling her back.

It had been agreed, Larry would remain in California and move to Los Angeles and live with Bill Waverly. Both seemed happy with this arrangement. Larry was now nearly 17 and could attend UCLA after high school. He dreamed of attending Cal Tech in nearby Pasadena for graduate study, intending to become an engineer. For Bill it was almost like having his late friend back again, and with Shorty moving out, he had lots of room.

So it was Evelyn Waverly found herself reversing the journey she started so long ago. She had no misgivings about returning to Detroit. She had grown up there, knew the area, and still assumed friends from high school would be there. Besides, between her savings and Shorty's income they should do well. There would still be separations and road trips, but at least they were now properly married and that made up for it. When the train pulled into Michigan Central, she was excited for this new beginning. The first thing they would have to locate was a place to stay.

Corktown with its close proximity to the ballpark and the railway station seemed a good place to look for a house. The neighborhood seemed quiet and tidy. There were a few restaurants nearby and Most Holy Trinity just up the street between Bagley and Porter streets. It had everything they needed. They soon located a bungalow on a shady street and purchased it. Two days later, Shorty reported for work with the Tigers. In his first outing he came out of the bullpen in the 5th inning and learned that Big League hitters were better than the competition he faced in semi-pro ball. He got roughed up pretty good that first day. But he grew more comfortable with each passing day until finally he was showing the talent that had brought him there in the first place.

The Corktown neighbors all seemed friendly enough and in the first few days of their residence Evelyn met most of them. She especially liked Mrs. Keillor who lived by herself in a house directly across the street. Her home was very well maintained with a fresh coat of paint and a new roof. In the small garage adjoining the house Evelyn noticed a late model Ford that looked like it was seldom driven. Mrs. Keillor insisted Evelyn call her Mona. In time they grew to be good friends. Many an afternoon would be spent taking coffee at Mona Keillor's kitchen table especially when Shorty was away. Mona appeared to be in her mid-60s. She was a widow, she said, and her only son was living in Europe doing some kind of government work. Mona knew of course, that her son was a fugitive, but she didn't know exactly where or why. She suspected some criminal intrigue but would not allow herself to speculate. Her safety had depended on her ignorance. The Europe cover story was a ruse suggested by Patrick to cover his trail. From time to time Mona would receive word through Father

Fleming, the pastor of Most Holy Trinity, about her son's wellbeing and the births of her grandchildren. The priest would pass such information to Mona behind the veil of the confessional. Fleming had been a boyhood friend of Patrick and Clancy and was completely trustworthy.

Evelyn and Shorty lived happily and comfortably for several years. Shorty's career was going well. In 1939, the couple welcomed a daughter and a son the year after, Mona was always happy to help with the babies. Evelyn had lost her own mother, Alice, years before so Mona assumed the role of grandmother to Evelyn's children. All was well in their little world. Even the outbreak of war in Europe did not diminish their bright prospects.

Everything changed overnight after Pearl Harbor. Shorty joined the Marines, his promising career put on indefinite hold. Larry, on the west coast had joined the Navy. So Evelyn found herself alone with two infants, living with the constant fear for the safety for her loved ones. If it had not been for Mona, Evelyn could not have made it.

Evelyn and Mona followed the news daily. Shorty was in Europe and Larry somewhere in the South Pacific. On the home front, people tried to maintain good spirits and live as normally as possible. In California, Bill Waverly had devoted himself to making patriotic films encouraging people to buy war bonds, and to conserve commodities for military use. Evelyn went to work at the Willow Run plant, along with legions of other women, turning out the iconic Liberator heavy bombers at astonishing rates. At the peak of the war effort the plant was producing one airplane an hour around the clock, each assembled from several million parts. Evelyn was proud of her role in this massive undertaking. She would reflect that each completed aircraft hastened the day when her loved ones could return from far away theaters of war and resume their lives. Mona Keillor did her part by caring for the children allowing Evelyn to work. Life was not easy but there was a community spirit, a feeling of togetherness that would see them through these dark days.

Shorty had landed on Omaha beach on D-Day and Larry, aboard the carrier Enterprise, piloted an F4F Wildcat fighter/escort at the pivotal battles of Midway and Leyte Gulf that shattered the enemy fleet and tightened the noose on Japan. Evelyn still lived in daily dread of a terrible telegram from the war office. Thank God it never came.

Then came the glorious news of V-E followed by V-J. The country erupted in euphoria of relief and thanksgiving. The war was over at last. This was followed shortly by even better news. Shorty and Larry were safe and were coming home! Larry and Bill Waverly wired they would come to Detroit for a reunion with Evelyn and her family. They would arrive two days before Shorty and would be there to surprise him when he arrived on September 30, at Michigan Central.

This was followed by even more good news. Father Fleming had informed Mona that Patrick, her son, would be coming to visit her. Coincidentally, he would be arriving at Michigan Central on the same day, September 30, as Shorty. She shared this happy news with Evelyn and it was immediately agreed Mona would accompany the family on the day of arrival.

Bill Waverly and Larry Donnelly arrived at Michigan Central on the 28th. Bill's eyes filled with joyful tears at the sight of his grandchildren. Larry and Evelyn embraced with even more tears. It was a moment of joy they all knew would be repeated with Shorty's arrival two days later. On September 30, three quarters of an hour before the arrival from New York of the Super Chief carrying Shorty, and an hour before the arrival of the Cannonball from St Louis carrying Patrick Keillor, the assembled family waited expectantly on the platform. Bill Waverly, Larry, Evelyn, her two children, and Mona Keillor along with Father Fleming waiting in joyful anticipation.

Shorty arrived on time and his tall frame was immediately visible over the heads of the milling crowd. He broke into a run when he saw the gathering waiting there for him and he seemed to enfold his family in an urgent lingering embrace. The joyful chaos continued uninterrupted for 20 minutes. Only Mona heard the announcement of the arrival of the train from St Louis.

Patrick Keillor was not expecting a welcoming committee. He thought perhaps Father Fleming or Mona, maybe both. So he was taken completely by surprise when he saw Mona, tears streaming down her face, surrounded by a crowd of strangers, all laughing, crying and embracing. Introductions were quickly made and Patrick greeted them all courteously but also warily. He had never seen them before and years of living anonymously had made him suspicious.

To Evelyn he seemed familiar, something about the searching look in his eye that reminded her of someone. She thought they might have met but could not imagine where or when. The man removed a handkerchief from his jacket pocket and gave it to Mona who dabbed her brimming eyes. It was only when Patrick took a seat on a bench, opened his brown leather valise, and withdrew the envelope filled with letters and photos for Mona that she knew.

"My God!" she gasped. "My God! It's you!"

Patrick made the connection more slowly. But finally he looked back at Evelyn and Larry with recognition. He was stunned into silence. He held out his hand to Evelyn. "Happy to meet you. How have you been?" He added wryly: "What a small world"

The tracks that intersect at Michigan Central Station diverge in every direction; but paths once crossed, may be bent by fate to join again. For Patrick, Evelyn, and Larry the circle once opened has closed. Castaways they were; ricocheting off the hard surface of circumstance, but drawn to reunion, in the invisible web of destiny.

Whistle Stop 5

OCTOBER 2, 1932

The Candidate

The special campaign train bearing the Democratic nominee for President pulled into Michigan Central at 11:15 AM on a Sunday morning threatening rain. The crowd awaiting the arrival of New York Governor Franklin Roosevelt milled around the platform excitedly. A band played "Anchors Aweigh" in recognition of Roosevelt's former role as Assistant Secretary of the Navy during the Great War, A few of the spectators waved signs and banners. The first off the train were the nominee's daughter and daughter-in-law. The two women chatted pleasantly with some of the assembled on lookers. Shortly after, the candidate's wife,

Eleanor, appeared and was acknowledged by the crowd. This was to be a frantically fast, twelve hour visit on the last stop of an arduous tour of the western states. Crowded into that space were three scheduled events, a luncheon and reception at the Statler Hotel, followed by a major speech at the Armory. Eleanor would end the day as guest of honor at an afternoon tea. The whole family was tired. Despite the grueling pace, they managed to appear fresh and energetic to the assembly of well-wishers. Since September, the Campaign Express had logged over 9000 miles and the candidate had delivered speeches or made appearances at every whistle stop along the way. Following this frenetic Detroit visit, the campaign would return to Albany for some welcome and much needed rest. Eleanor was anxious to keep everything on schedule so hurriedly directed the ladies to the waiting limousines. The candidate himself had not yet appeared, still in the family Pullman car, requiring a little extra time to prepare himself. Finally the Governor appeared supported by his son John. Franklin exuded a lively, cheerful manner that belied the ravages of the crippling disease that had taken the use of his legs. He appeared the picture of manly vigor and confidence. He seemed the embodiment of the lyrics of his campaign theme song: "Happy Days Are Here Again."

The route to the hotel was lined with cheering crowds and more than a few, disinterested, merely curious, bystanders. Nearly everyone watching the motorcade was hurting during these hard times. Most were investing their remaining hopes that Roosevelt was the man who could fix the horrible national disaster of the Depression. A few, more cynical, had given up hope altogether. Roosevelt would have to address the concerns of both audiences.

During the luncheon, an accompanying orchestra performed jaunty music mostly ignored by the guests as they finished their meals. The conversations at each table revolved around politics, mostly local. A few expressed concern about unrest in far-away Europe. The orchestra struck up a new tune written especially for the campaign:

"Four long years we've had misunderstanding
And we have all felt so strange
We sure need a change
And the good times we now are demanding
For Hoover caused us unrest
He failed when put to the test"

Roosevelt with Frank Murphy, the mayor of Detroit, sat at the head table. The two discussed the disastrous state of the automotive industry crippling the local economy. Automobile production had fallen by 75 percent since the crash. Tar paper shacks had sprung up around the city where the impoverished waited desperately for relief. Breadlines provided hungry people scant nourishment. The overnight slums bred resentment and despair that would surely lead to lawlessness. "Hooverville" became the name of these pockets of misery. It got so bad that railroad coal men had taken to shoveling lumps of fuel from passing trains to provide warmth for the destitute to collect beside the tracks. "Buddy can you spare a dime?" became the anthem of the era.

"We'll try somebody else
You'll try somebody else
And if we do we'll not feel blue
And then we'll prosper again"

President and Republican candidate Herbert Hoover had insisted that the Depression was a momentary aberration. He depended upon the basics; self-reliance and confidence in American businesses, to inevitably set things right. The "Invisible Hand" of the market place and a little patience, were all that was needed. Earlier that year, a group of distressed farmers had gone to Washington to convey their needs to the President. Hoover insisted they were a little late in their appeal since the Depression had ended six months before.

"So we'll try somebody else
And that somebody else
Is Franklin D
Just wait and see
And we'll all be happy again"

One of the most divisive issues of the campaign had been the repayment of bonuses the government had promised to veterans of the Great War. These payments had been deferred by law until 1945. But people simply could not wait that long. In summer of 1932 the situation came to a dangerous head. An army of veterans and other discontented, roughly 40,000 strong, converged on Washington demanding redress. Hoover would not give in out of concern for breaking the budget. When violence broke out two marchers were wounded fatally by police. Hoover ordered Army units led by Chief of Staff General Douglas McArthur, to clear the protestor's camp. Two officers in his command were notable: Dwight Eisenhower and George Patton. When the military finally attacked, supported by six light tanks a crowd of onlookers shouted "Shame!" "Shame!" The terrible affair doomed Hoover's campaign. But Roosevelt remained on the fence over the controversy. The Detroit press had asked for his thoughts on the issue but Roosevelt side stepped, insisting he was not yet ready to declare his views. That in itself became a banner headline in the *Detroit Free Press* the next day.

"R double O-S-E
Then V-E-L-T
That's the way his name is spelt
It's Franklin D
For you and me
And we'll all be happy again!"

Since the Civil War only two Democrats had served as president, Woodrow Wilson, and Grover Cleveland. For the most part, the maxim expressed by President Calvin Coolidge: "the business of America is business" held sway over the thinking of the American electorate. Government was seen as an intruder in American life; not a benevolent participant. The belief in hard work and self-reliance, unencumbered by government interference was thought to be the true source of American greatness. Charity was seen as an individual moral imperative but not a governmental responsibility. But this philosophy was being deeply challenged by the travail of the Great Depression. The South, which still harbored resentment from the Civil War, could be depended upon to vote Democratic since they blamed the Republican Party for Reconstruction. Roosevelt's ambition was to broaden his appeal under the banner of his "New Deal" which he promised at his nominating convention in Chicago that summer. He went about forging a broad coalition in support of his vision. The proper role of government, he argued, was to help create greater equality of opportunity while weaving a durable social safety net. If fully realized, this initiative would eliminate poverty from the nation. American politics, and more broadly American society; for better or for worse, would never be the same. The Great Debate continues to this day.

After the luncheon, Roosevelt retired to the presidential suite to rest and finish preparation of his speech to be given at the armory later that afternoon. His motorcade enroute drew another throng of onlookers. The same faces, the same pain, the same hopes. Roosevelt began his remarks that day noting it was inappropriate to speak of politics on the Sabbath. He intended instead to reflect on Government, which in his view was not the same thing. He expanded on two opposing currents in American society. Those who wish to "leave it alone" and depend on the irresistible force of markets to eventually solve the nation's problems; versus those who could not wait and demanded action. He spoke of those who viewed prosperity as a result of a "rising tide" lifting all, versus the belief that the surplus of the wealthy would inevitably "trickle down" to those below. When he concluded his remarks he apologized that he had given more of a sermon than a speech which he said after all, was more appropriate for the Sabbath.

As his train pulled out of Michigan Central that evening, Roosevelt felt buoyed by the positive response he got from the crowds in Detroit. But a shadow of lingering doubt troubled him. The crowds had been smaller than hoped for today. What could this mean? Was the electorate at this late moment of the campaign swinging back to the familiar orthodoxy of the past? Was his message of an activist government and a New Deal starting to fall on deaf ears? Were people desperate enough to try something new and different? He thought of all the stops he had made, all across this enormous troubled land. He could see it everywhere he went. The hopes, fears, and doubts of scared people. He was a man of enormous self-confidence, but the gravity of the task at hand unnerved and humbled him. In the back of his mind was the flicker of fear that his infirmity in the end would best him and all his ambitions. As the train rumbled on through the darkness towards his unknown destiny he fell into a fitful sleep. His future was in the hands of fate and the voters.

Whistle Stop 6

JUNE 8, 1926

The Babe

The 8:50 AM Cleveland Mercury, pride of the New York Central Railway, roared westward hugging the shore of Lake Erie bound for Detroit. It was delivering the New York Yankees for an afternoon game, start of a four game series with the Tigers. On board was a pantheon of Yankee deity: Gehrig, Lazzeri, Combs, future Hall of Famers all, and the redoubtable Babe Ruth. Along with Koenig and Meusel, this lineup constituted the dreaded Murderer's Row that tormented American League pitching through much of the 1920's. The team was in a sullen mood after dropping 2 out of 3 in Cleveland and was anxious to right the ship against Detroit which was struggling, playing .500 ball. The players mostly sat staring out the windows, watching the monotonous scenery rush by. Eventually, a card game broke out, low stakes, as most of the players were frugal. The money they earned was outstanding for the time but not so extravagant to prevent them from seeking employment during the off-season. Babe scowled over his 3rd schooner of beer and opened another pack of cigarettes. "Goddam, I'm bored" he bellowed. Gehrig shot a glance and a wink at Combs who smiled faintly, The Babe was getting buzzed. Bad news for the Tigers.

George Herman "Babe" Ruth (aka The Bambino, aka the Sultan of Swat) was as much a symbol of an era as he was an icon of sport. He was one of the nation's first mega celebrities. He was the object of adoration for every boy and teenager in the country. Whenever he came to town, crowds would pour into the streets hoping to catch a glimpse of their hero or the most treasured prize of all: an autograph. He could fill to capacity any big league stadium where he appeared and even the home town fans would lustily cheer his exploits. When confronted by a reporter (obviously not a sports fan) chastising him for being paid more than the president he shot back, "Why not, I'm having a better year than him". Loud, profane, genial, a man of enormous appetites and legendary vices, he was a one man traveling road show. And that show would be playing in Detroit for the next four days.

Even his detractors admitted that he had a big heart to match his out size personality. He seldom denied autographs and could often be found in a crowd of boys enthralling them with his presence and passing out souvenirs. It was very clear he loved being Babe Ruth. The dimensions of his stardom inspired legends that added to his fame. It was said he once visited a sick young fan in hospital and promised to whack a home run in his honor. And then at the ball park that very afternoon, delivered. And then there was the immortal "called shot" in the 5th inning of game three of the 32 World Series at Wrigley Field. Both stories are indelibly written in baseball lore whether they happened or not. But that was all in the future.

For the present, not the Babe himself nor his legions of fans could predict the entry he would write into history this day in Navin Field against the home town Tiger's nine.

The train slowed as it approached Michigan Central Station. Of all the railway stations in the country, and the Babe had seen them all, Detroit was one of his favorites because of the jumbo hot dogs sold there; thick, juicy, seared on the grill, piled high with onions, pickle relish, slathered in mustard and pillowed on a toasted bun. This was the Babe's preferred pregame meal. The vendor who sold these gluttonous treats occupied a corner tucked between a stairway and the telegraph desk. His original store in nearby Hamtramck had been so successful he had expanded into the railroad station several years ago. Babe Ruth became his most famous, if not most frequent customer. Ruth exited the train carrying his luggage and headed straight for this location trailing a quickly growing throng of men and boys behind him. On a good day when he was hungry he could polish off three jumbo dogs. Today he was not that hungry. A crowd of youngsters gathered as he bellied up to the bar and placed his order. Only one. The cook, mildly disappointed, quickly filled his order. Ruth turned and waved expansively to the crowd and shook a few hands with mustard stained fingers. No matter, the Babe was in town!

After his snack in the railroad station, Ruth would customarily proceed to the ballpark and feast on Tiger pitching. He would go on in his career to hit 60 home runs at Detroit, more than any other visiting team player. He would club his 700th home run there. But again, those heroics were all in the future. Today's entry into the history books would be remembered as one equally impressive. For today in the third inning the Babe would swat the longest home run ever hit in Detroit; the longest home run Babe Ruth ever hit; maybe the longest home run ever hit by anyone, anytime.

In the locker room before the game the players gathered in small groups discussing all the minutiae of interest to ball players on game day; the peculiarities of Navin Field, the strengths and weaknesses of the Tiger lineup. The Babe, because of his diet, was renowned for prodigious belching and flatulence. When asked a question by Lazeeri about the Tigers bullpen Ruth looked thoughtful for a moment then offered a loud gassy reply. The locker room erupted in raucous laughter. Babe Ruth had a knack for keeping things loose.

In the 3rd inning, already leading 4-1 and with Gehrig on base, the Babe crushed a Lil Stoner pitch and sent it in a towering arc towards Trumball Avenue. Ty Cobb, the Tigers skipper, reported after the game he had watched the ball fly overhead from his position in center field and never saw a ball sail further. It flew over the stadium fence and struck a parked car outside. It took a big bounce and continued to roll down the street with a hoard of fans in hot pursuit. The papers reported that when the ball was retrieved it had traveled some 800 feet from home plate. The "official" distance, the article stated, was a mind numbing 626 feet, more than two football fields. Lacking the precision of modern technology the reported distance can be viewed today with some skepticism. However far it traveled, there can be no doubt it was a mighty blow.

The Babe was not through for the day. The Tigers came back to tie the game in the 9th forcing extra innings. So in the top of the 11th with Gehrig on, Babe Ruth did it again powering a home run into the stands, not as spectacularly as his earlier blast, but much more decisively. The Yankees won the game 11-9 and went on to sweep the series. The traveling road show was ready to move on to St Louis for a three game series.

After the last game of the series, the Yankees hurried back to the rail station to catch the 4:15 to St. Louis on the Wabash Cannon Ball. They had to hurry to make it. There was barely time for the Babe to polish off a single hot dog. A reporter from the Free Press, trying to get a quote for the late edition pursued him down the platform and shouted a question about how he had played so well. Ruth paused and replied impishly "Its simple kids, if you eat, and smoke, and drink, and screw as much as me; well kiddos, someday you'll be as good at sports". Babe Ruth gave out a great bellow of laughter and with a wink boarded the train.

Whistle Stop 7

MAY 04, 1917

The Entertainer

"Pack up your troubles in your old kit bag
And Smile, Smile, Smile..
While I am missing you across the miles
Smile boys that's the style
What's the use of worrying?
It never was worthwhile
So pack up your troubles in your old kit bag
And Smile, Smile, Smile"

Oleda Joule sat on a mahogany bench in the middle of the Main Waiting Room. Unconsciously her fingers danced over an invisible keyboard in accompaniment to the jaunty little tune. She raised her voice loudly and belted out the chorus: Smile, Smile, Smile. The brass band in one corner of the terminal was entertaining the crowds rushing through a busy Friday morning. The station had arranged this concert to reduce the stress of the throngs of travelers. The hope was the music would calm the frayed nerves of people rushing about on tight schedules. So the band offered cheerfully patriotic and light hearted ditties. The travelers rushed by without stopping long to listen. On any weekday morning a big crowd was normal, but since war had been declared, the traffic volume was overwhelming. Large numbers of young men catching trains to go off to war and their despondent sweethearts and mothers were on hand to see them off. There was a buzz of anticipation in the air, along with a heavy dose of apprehension. After the long tension of waiting, it was a relief that now the question of whether America would go to war, was decided. But there was also a vague foreboding, as so many left home, many for the first time, towards a dangerous mission and an uncertain future. There was a "Let's get on with it mood"; mixed with a bluster of bravado from untested soldiers. "We'll bag Kaiser Bill, and hang him from the nearest tree". Such was the range of emotion that filled the railway station this morning. Oleda viewed it all with a barely contained excitement.

Many of the soon-to-be soldiers were headed for basic training in one of several locations in the South. These were noticeable for their lack of uniforms. They were a brawny lot for the most part, Italian, Polish, Greek, Irish, native sons; sons of immigrants. The black men remained separated in a group by themselves; all bound for Army induction since the Marines barred them and the Navy greatly restricted their service. Nearly all the waiting men were veterans of Detroit's many assembly lines. Now they would have to learn the skills of another kind of line, one bordered by barbed wire. The wrench and screwdriver of their trade would be replaced by the hand tools of war, the rifle and grenade. Now the only product of their mass production would be enemy bodies. These grim facts were not completely understood by the men waiting to board the southbound trains. But they would learn quickly. Other soldiers, already in uniform were ready to ship out and they stood in long lines waiting to board eastbound trains. Docks up and down the coast anxiously awaited this human tide. Oleda Joule would be boarding an east bound train. She was shipping out on the Olympic for Europe. This feisty 19 year old wisp of a girl from Marine City Michigan, was going to war.

Oleda was a very accomplished young woman. She was trained as a telephone operator. She was also a talented musician. She played the piano for dance bands in various venues in Michigan's thumb region ever since she was thirteen. She had been a dedicated student. In an era when education beyond elementary was unusual for girls, she was a high school graduate, the only one in her class of nine. After school she had been given a job by Bell Telephone training other young women to become operators. It was this skill that was needed by the military and she enlisted as a volunteer to help set up and run a communications network for General Pershing's AEF headquarters in Chaumont, France. Upon her arrival in Detroit, Oleda was immediately impressed at the vastness of Michigan Central and the pounding energy of so many people in motion. She had a sense of embarking on a great adventure as she sat there awaiting her train.

The train ride to Newark was long and tedious. The scenery passing by the window of her rail car gradually grew monotonous until it was too dark to see much more than the lights of farmhouses they passed. She found herself dozing off, her head rolling on her shoulders. An occasional jar from the train tracks would snap her neck upright and she would waken and yawn before nodding off again. Certainly not the best night's sleep she had ever had. Each time the train stopped a fresh load of soldiers boarded until there was barely room to stand in the car. Oleda did share seating with four nurses who were also bound for France. She was happy to hear they were also sailing on the Olympic so she would have company on the long voyage. Several of the male passengers thought to try their luck with the unaccompanied females, but it never went past innocent flirtation. After all, on a crowded train it was impossible to find a place to be alone for a little romance.

Oleda had grown up on the shores of the Great Lakes. She was no stranger to vast bodies of water. The thought of crossing the wide ocean did not bother her. After all, if you could not see across it, then the view was the same, ocean or lake. So what was the difference? What did impress her when they finally arrived at the docks was the ship itself. The Olympic was designed to carry passengers on the trans-Atlantic voyage with speed and comfort. It had been built as a sister vessel to the ill-fated Titanic, whose tragic sinking had shocked the world five years before. Since her childhood, she had watched the seasonal passage of freight-carrying ships ply the waters of the Great Lakes. By comparison they looked clumsy and unglamorous next to the sleek profile of the Olympic. Even outfitted as a troop carrier and stripped of many of her former luxuries, she was still a beautiful ship. Oleda and her companion nurses were assigned a cabin that formerly would have accommodated second class passengers. It was crowded but very clean. Since the women thought it ill advised to be too visible among a shipload of men, they mostly stayed out of sight.

The difference between the Great Lakes and the ocean became apparent to Oleda on the morning of the second day. The seas were heavy with rolling swells that bobbed the enormous ship like an apple in a barrel. Then she and many others were forced to the deck. Mercifully the rolling stopped overnight and they awoke to calm seas. After her unpleasant bout of sea sickness she started to view the voyage in a less favorable light. She began to look forward to their arrival and return to dry land. Her recollection of recent at sea disasters did not help. She thought of Titanic and nervously scanned the sea, alert for icebergs in their path. Then there was the terror that sunk the Lusitania. She could imagine a menacing pack of U boats trailing them like wolves. But the rest of the voyage went smoothly and they arrived in Southampton none the worse for wear.

After the discomfort of the voyage they were not prepared for the gross inconvenience of what followed. The Spanish flu pandemic required them to remain on board in quarantine for two weeks. After the nervous tension of the voyage, no one was prepared for the utter tedium of inactivity. Oleda wrote letters to everyone back home- her family, friends, her pastor, and her school principal, just to help fill the time. Eventually, all the women, out of sheer boredom, began to venture out from their cabin to wander the ship. That is how Oleda discovered the grand piano in the large space that used to be the ship's ballroom, converted now to a mess deck. Apparently it was a fixture when the Olympic was a passenger ship. Oleda wondered if it had been left on purpose or simply forgotten. No matter, she was going to play. She ignored the large group of soldiers sitting at tables, talking, playing cards, drinking coffee. She sat before the gleaming keyboard and her fingers danced over the polished ivory keys. It felt so good…

"Over there; over there
Send the word; Send the word
Over there
That the Yanks are coming
The Yanks are coming
The drums rum-tumming everywhere
So prepare; say a prayer
Send the word; send the word to beware
Over, we're coming over
And we won't come back
Till its over, over there"

She paused when she noticed the buzz of conversation had subsided. They were listening to her. She resumed playing and the men were now singing lustily. When she finished, the audience began to cheer and Oleda noticed a large crowd of new arrivals was gathering. The playing cards and coffee cups were now abandoned. She acknowledged their ovation and immediately started another tune:

> "It's a long way to Tipperary
> It's a long way to go
> It's a long way to Tipperary
> To the sweetest girl I know..
> Goodbye Piccadilly
> Farewell Leicester Square
> It's a long, long way to Tipperary
> But my heart lies there"

Oleda continued her impromptu concert late into the evening. She would respond to requests from the audience who raised their voices to sing along. She played mostly jaunty tunes that seemed to rouse her audience. *"Oh! You Beautiful Doll"*, *"K-K-K-Katy"*, *"Oh! How I Hate to Get Up in the Morning"*. When she launched into *"Mademoiselle from Armentieres"* the audience roared with great gusto: 'Hinky-Dinky Parley voo" at the end of each verse. Late in the evening she switched to a more sentimental mood. *"After the War is Over"*, *"Waltzing Matilda"*, *"There's a Long, Long Trail A-Winding"*, *"Rose of Picardy"*, *and "Auld Lang Syne"*. When she left the piano there was not a dry eye in the place.

The quarantine lasted another tiresome week but she was in the mess deck every night performing for the troops. At the end of that time she was asked to join the Red Cross to permanently entertain the camps and hospitals. But Oleda had other duty. She had come to France to work on the telephones and that was what she intended to do.

Oleda Joule would fulfill her assigned mission in France. She was part of the staff at General Pershing's headquarters till the war ended. After that time she remained in France for a year following the Armistice to help make arrangements for soldiers going home. After the war she returned home to Michigan. For many years after she continued her career for the phone company and played piano professionally throughout Michigan. To the end of her life she enjoyed playing the songs from the Great War. When history was written many stories were told about that dreadful conflict. The books remembered the doughboys who had charged across no-man's land with bullets whizzing and bombs bursting. They recalled those dashing pilots who took to the sky in flimsy air ships to battle Von Richthofen's Flying Circus. But Oleda did something important too, unremembered as it was by the history books. She gave lonely soldiers a long way from home for a few fleeting moments, a reason to pack up their troubles and smile. She had sparked a flicker of happiness to illuminate the dim twilight of war.

"Pack up your troubles in your old kit bag
And Smile, Smile, Smile.
While I am missing you across the miles
Smile boys that's the style
What's the use of worrying?
It never was worthwhile
So pack up your troubles in your old kit bag
And Smile, Smile, Smile

Over there; over there
Send the word; Send the word
Over there
That the Yanks are coming
The Yanks are coming
The drums rum-tumming everywhere
So prepare; say a prayer
Send the word; send the word to beware
Over, we're coming over
And we won't come back
Till its over, over there

It's a long way to Tipperary
It's a long way to go
It's a long way to Tipperary
To the sweetest girl I know..
Goodbye Pickadilly
Farewell Leicester Square
It's a long, long way to Tipperary
But my heart lies there"

Whistle Stop 8

APRIL 22, 1932

The Artist

The *Detroit Free Press* article reported that Senor Diego Rivera's arrival in Detroit at Michigan Central Station was something of a milestone for him. The front page column noted waggishly that this was the first time the artist had been on time for anything. Characteristically, he would arrive late for appointments during his many world travels. From New York, to Paris, Mexico City to Moscow, he was known for tardiness and this became a trademark of his eccentric persona. This time the train was on time and so was he. Among his other peculiarities, he was a man well known for prodigious appetites for food, drink, and carnality. He was the father of numerous illegitimate offspring. Despite his obvious weaknesses of the flesh, he was internationally recognized for his artistic vision and his magnificent frescoes which graced galleries in New York, San Francisco, Spain, Italy, and his native Mexico City. It was this talent that brought Rivera to Detroit. Edsel Ford, auto magnate and scion of the Ford family was an active patron of the arts. He had offered Rivera a commission to paint two murals in the Garden Court of the magnificent Detroit Institute of Art on Woodward Avenue. The nonspecific theme for the work would be a tribute to Detroit industry which was the marvel of the industrial age. Of all the sanctuaries of capitalism, Detroit was its most sacred temple. Rivera admitted he would seek inspiration for his composition by visiting as many local factories as possible. He was similarly fascinated by the bridges, tunnels, and skyscrapers of this Midwestern metropolis.

Despite his talent and reputation, Rivera was a controversial choice for the project. First and foremost, he was a foreigner of Mexican birth. He was a self-proclaimed atheist which was certain to offend community sensibilities. His libertine lifestyle was distasteful to many. Lastly and most disturbing of all, he was member of the Mexican communist party. He had sojourned in the Soviet Union for an extended visit in the late 1920's where he picked up some mastery of the Russian language. The artist's proletariat viewpoint would undoubtedly be the filter through which his depiction of capitalism would be presented. Capturing the dignity and solidarity of men at work without brooding over the dehumanizing regimentation of factory life would be a daunting artistic challenge. A less talented artist or a more suspicious patron might never have undertaken such a commission. A foreign born, atheist, communist, no matter how admired his art, would have many local biases to overcome to achieve acceptance. The extenuating circumstance of his employer being a titan of industry was an ironic footnote.

Rivera stepped off the train onto the platform accompanied by his wife, Frieda Kahlo, herself an artist of growing renown. The couple had met at art school and she was now Diego's third wife, but the lusty artist had so many mistresses it was difficult to keep track. Frida, for her part, was known for her extra marital affairs as well, but provided an otherwise stark contrast to Diego. She was 20 years younger than her husband and presented a slim appearance next to her burly spouse. She might have easily been mistaken as the daughter of this middle-aged man. The couple had a tumultuous relationship which resulted in their eventual divorce and then, remarriage which would last until her death. Diego would, true to form, marry again after Frida's passing. Late in life Rivera acknowledged that Frida had been the great love of his life. Despite their mutual infidelity they seemed to sincerely love each other, joined as they were by their art. On this spring morning they beamed warmly as they joined a large reception party gathered to greet them. The Detroit Free Press noted her dark hair was parted and drawn into pigtails tied with bows which gave her a girlish appearance the paper found fetching. She carried in her hands a ukulele; presumably she did not trust to the possession of careless porters who might scratch it.

One of those gathered on the platform stood out in the crowd. He was a giant man, nearly 300 pounds and half a head taller than most of the rest of the crowd. His name was Kola Kwariani and he was a professional wrestler well known in Detroit's sporting world. His professional name was Nick the Wrestler and he was scheduled on the card that very evening at the Olympia arena. He had made the trip this afternoon to Michigan Central hoping for a chance to meet his idol, the famous artist. Kola was a man nearly as colorful and accomplished as Rivera himself. He had been born in Russia and had immigrated to the United States three years before. He was bilingual, and an amateur painter of some small acclaim. He would in future years become close friends of the movie director Stanley Kubrick who cast him in several early movies. His most unusual passion however was the game of chess in which he was acknowledged as an expert. This cerebral pastime was a stark contrast to his day job of eye gouging and body slamming. Nick would come to a violent end nearly 50 years later when he was attacked by a gang of five young hooligans while leaving his chess club in New York City. Even at his advanced age he was a formidable figure but there were simply too many of the assailants to overcome and he was beaten badly. He died later in hospital at age 77. Today, Kola grinned with pleasure when introduced to his hero. Kola told Rivera how well known and admired Rivera was in Russia from his time spent there. The two enjoyed a cordial conversation in Russian and Kola was described as beaming when he left the scene, his bald, grizzly and cauliflower eared countenance almost boyishly transformed.

Rivera would in the ensuing months complete the overall design of his masterpiece and go on to complete the work itself. The technique for painting a fresco was to first apply plaster to the wall and then paint with watercolor on the still wet surface. This necessitated completing only small parts of the composition at one time. The following day, more plaster would be applied and the painting would continue. When the plaster finally dried this gave the frescoes an ethereal quality of emerging from deep within the wall rather than being applied upon it. When the painting was finally completed it elicited the controversy that was anticipated from the outset. There were nude figures. "Scandalous!" critics thundered. There was a symbolic depiction of the Nativity. "Profanity!" the clergy shouted. Offensive to some was the depiction of white and black workers side by side on the assembly line in apparent solidarity and equality. "Never!" they silently vowed. The city's first major episode of racial unrest was still a decade away. Sadly, the seeds that would eventually germinate violence had already been planted in fertile ground many years before. The contagion of racism had infected the workplace and would eventually spawn an epidemic of racial unrest that would flare up during the years to come.

The grip of the Great Depression had not yet loosened as Rivera completed his masterwork and many families were still struggling. This was especially true for a large community of Mexican expatriates who had fallen on hard times in the Motor City. They had been lured to Detroit by the prospect of good wages in the automotive industry. For most the promised prosperity was not delivered. Now they were stranded and wished to return home. Their plight became known to Rivera while he was completing the work at the DIA. He proposed an innovative solution. If the manufacturing sector of the United States could not absorb even the native population looking for work, why not arrange transport for Mexican nationals to return to Mexico? The agricultural sector of the Mexican economy was heavily dependent upon labor and Rivera argued convincingly that the refugees could find work in their homeland. Beyond that, the appeal of returning to Mexico was irresistible even patriotic. In any case the situation in Michigan was so desperate that something had to be done. Soon thousands of displaced families had signed up to participate in this relocation. Train transportation, originating from several locations in Michigan, including Michigan Central, would proceed to Southern terminus in either El Paso or Laredo where they would meet officials from several Mexican States. There they would arrange repatriation for these refugees and transportation to agricultural colonies south of the border. Those who could qualify were given homestead rights to land in Mexico. The journey was completed nonstop over a grueling forty hours on the train.

History is mostly silent on the fate which befell those who participated in this exodus. It is known that some of the refugees succeeded quite well while others fared no better in their homeland then they had in Michigan. Reading the journals of the time it is hard not to conclude that the removal of Mexicans from the Motor City was motivated more by political and economic concerns than humanitarian ones, however sincere Rivera's original motives were.

The controversy surrounding the Detroit Industry murals has long since subsided. The frescoes are now nearly universally admired as a powerful example of 20th century art and attract thousands of visitors annually to visit the Garden Courtyard to study and revel in this epic theme. As much as anything, the work captures a particular point in time that will not return. One cannot help wonder the result if a modern artist was asked to paint an updated version of the subject. The work done by Diego Rivera, however, remains as an enduring symbol of one of the most consequential artists of his day. Despite his controversial, somewhat unsavory life style, he created a legacy we still admire today.

Author's footnote: In November of 2019 a visit to Budapest coincided with a major exhibition of the paintings of Frieda Kahlo at the National Museum of Art. This world class exhibition space is housed in the old Imperial Palace built imposingly on the Buda hills overlooking the Danube. The line to be admitted to the exhibition stretched outside and halfway around the massive building. We were amazed when we learned all these people had already purchased tickets but still had to wait in line to gain admission. Clearly the crowd thought the event was important and worth the wait.

Whistle Stop 9

THE 1943 RIOT (PART 1) JOSHUA

From Mound Bayou Mississippi to Detroit 1935

It had been a very wet spring in Bolivar County. The bottom land that Cyrus Holloway sharecropped was prone to flooding even in years of normal rainfall and this year was way above average. The only thing growing in the fields was a bumper crop of thick clinging mud. Most of the tenants to the lands owned by Mr. Emmitt Prejean, the largest farmer in the vicinity of Mound Bayou, were already way behind in their planting. The season was barely beginning and yet the crop was already threatened.

If more normal conditions followed for the rest of the growing season, there might still be a crop to bring to market to pay the rent with enough left to keep Cyrus and his family alive for another year. This was the grueling reality of life for sharecroppers in Mississippi. Everything depended on a generous Providence giving what was needed in the right amount and at the right time. Cyrus knew better than to rely totally on Providence. He had his hopes dashed often enough to know that frequent prayer did not always sway the Almighty. Cyrus believed the Good Lord loved all his children but He seemed to love his white children just a little more and allocated most of the prosperity to them. Black people had to rely on hope that things would get better over time and Cyrus had been waiting a long time. Brother Franklin, the Baptist preacher whose backwoods church the Holloway family attended, liked to remind his congregation of the afflictions borne by the children of Israel and they were undoubtedly God's chosen people. So could there be any doubt of the favor God felt for his black children? Cyrus wished God was a little more generous with his blessings and a little less apt to convey His favor through adversity. Still like most men, living in constant apprehension of the future, he kept a copy of the Good Book near his bedside hoping God would notice. He might then be more favorably disposed to help him. Cyrus wasn't sure it helped, but he knew it couldn't hurt his prospects. His wife Harriet was constant in seeking comfort in the Bible and would read its verses daily. To be poor and black in the South you needed all the comfort you could get from any source.

Mr. Prejean was not known as a cruel landlord and was thought of as a reasonably fair man to deal with. But none of his tenants ever had any doubts about the limits of his benevolence. Two years before Mr. Prejean had evicted a white tenant who fell in arrears when his unfortunate wife had been stricken with cancer. The poor man had turned to the bottle to assuage his grief and Mr. Prejean had turned him out. Still it was known that he gave the man 50 dollars to help get him back on his feet. Among farmers in the South such generosity was not to be expected. But even a tolerant landlord expected his rents. Not surprisingly there was no similar story recalling his charity to a black tenant. The price you paid for falling behind in the rent was steep. And Cyrus Holloway made certain he would never pay that price.

The Holloway family consisted of four surviving children, fifteen year old Maya, sixteen year old Lucinda (known to the family as Lulu), eighteen year old Joshua, and twenty year old Clem. Clem was the only son of Cyrus's older brother George who had moved to Detroit several years before to find work on the assembly line with the Ford Motor Company. George's wife, Clem's mother, had passed away some years before. When George decided to move it was agreed it would be better for Clem to stay with his uncle Cyrus and family until his father found work and would send for him. That arrangement suited everyone including Clem who was agreeable to farm life. Even after two years he preferred to remain on the farm rather than join his father in the factory up north where the weather was cold and factory life was unappealing. Cyrus was glad for the extra hands so he was content with the arrangement. Harriet saw to the children's education and insisted the youngsters make the half mile walk to the schoolhouse in Mound Bayou when the load of farm work permitted it. She also made sure the family was present on Sundays at Brother Franklin's services and Sunday school. As a result they could all read and write; skills she treasured and put to use daily in studying Scripture. When the farm chores were most demanding, the whole family would work side by side in the fields, each performing tasks consistent with their ages and skills. Clem being the oldest would do most of the heavy work alongside his uncle. Joshua would usually man the plow and was very at good at it. He would walk for hours behind the mule cutting deep furrows in the earth till his back and feet ached. His rows were always straight and the optimal depth, following the contours of the land.

To pass the time Joshua would raise his voice in song as he plowed. He was blessed with a magnificent singing voice universally praised by anyone fortunate enough to hear it. He spanned the notes of his range from highest to lowest with ease and with perfect breath control. His voice was rich and his tones deep and resonant. He was the pride of the church choir in Mound Bayou and even white residents would come to worship on Sundays just to hear him sing, to the great satisfaction of Brother Franklin. It was Mr. Prejean himself upon hearing the talented young man had presented him an amazing gift. Prejean had a large collection of phonograph records which he would listen to for hours, reveling in the music, providing transport from the drudgery of daily living. He had acquired a recording of the song "Old Man River" from the Broadway production of *Show Boat* recorded by the famous bass singer Paul Robeson. This he presented to Josh. The Holloway family boasted no phonograph but one was found in Brother Franklin's church. Joshua was spellbound by the rich sonorous tones and aspired to follow the footsteps of the renowned singer. This song was quickly added to his growing repertoire. His cousin Clem was especially fond of the song and asked Josh to sing it frequently. For one so young he captured the pathos of the song brilliantly.

The struggling family managed the yearly cycles of farm life with no clear-cut view of what the future held. This particular spring a turning point arrived. A letter from Uncle George arrived at the post office in Mound Bayou addressed to Cyrus. He wrote that anyone on the farm who wished to join him could be assured a good living. Cyrus thought he detected a hint of loneliness in his brother's note, which pained him. George had always been a family man and his isolation living so far from home and family must have been difficult. Cyrus and Harriet discussed the matter after the dinner dishes were washed that very evening. It was agreed that one of the boys could be spared and should go but one would have to stay on. What was best for the children was the most important consideration. After that how each choice would impact the farm work was also discussed.

Cyrus admitted that Clem was a better farmer than Josh and liked the work better as well. Harriet for her part was thinking about Josh's great gift and wondered if the Good Lord was encouraging her son to go to the city to share his musical talent with a larger audience. As painful as the decision was it was agreed that Clem should remain on the farm and Josh be allowed to go to Detroit. If he could not find employment in music there were always good paying factory jobs to be had.

Once the decision was made the very difficult question arose as to how Josh would travel to Detroit. Cyrus could not afford to pay for the trip and it was way too far to walk. Harriet reminded Cyrus that runaway slaves from all over the south had followed the underground railway to freedom traveling mostly on foot. But that journey was no less dangerous in the Jim Crow South of the 1930s than it had been for runaways escaping the plantations before the Civil War. Then a solution was suggested by Brother Franklin. It was known that one of the biggest employers of black labor was the railroads, If Josh could secure a position as a Pullman Porter, he could ride the rails all the way to Detroit and be paid for it. If Mr. Prejean could be persuaded to recommend Josh it would help. When asked, Prejean's first thought was whether the land could still make rent with the loss of a male worker and he was reluctant to help. The Holloways were his most dependable tenants and he wanted to avoid the chance he might lose them. In the end he relented when he thought of that wonderful voice and its gift to the world. So it was arranged that Josh would be hired by the Pullman Company. Following the footsteps of his slave ancestors he turned to the North Star to seek a better life.

In the late summer of that year Josh Holloway found himself riding the Southern Constellation on its three times weekly journey from Mobile to Atlanta. Josh was assigned the menial duties of porter to the passengers. This mostly required transporting the baggage to and from the Pullman car, shining shoes, delivering coffee in the morning, opening windows in passenger compartments, making the bed in the evening and any other jobs seeing to the comfort of travelers. The club car where meals and drinks were served was staffed by a separate group of waiters. Since this occupation required more interaction with travelers it was thought to be a higher status; and due to occasional gratuities collected, a more lucrative position. Josh hoped someday to become a waiter.

The white passengers' behavior towards the help was more condescending than abusive. For the most part as prosperous southerners they were accustomed to domestic workers and were generally tolerant of their proximity if not appropriately grateful of their services. "Please" and "Thank you" were expressed to Josh occasionally but not frequently, and generally not heartfelt. Josh got along tolerably well with his frequent "Yes Sirs!", servile demeanor and avoidance of making any comments that might get him into trouble. Inside he seethed with resentment but he never let on. He bided his time. As an employee he could not choose the routes he served. He would need to be patient and alert for opportunities that would get him closer to Detroit. At least then he would be escaping the South.

Eventually his vocal talents were discovered by a conductor who heard Josh singing to himself one evening while cleaning an empty compartment. His boss sensed an opportunity and directed Josh to perform in the club car for the enjoyment of diners. He would station himself in an unoccupied corner next to a small piano on hand which the railway had installed for background music. Pianos were not a common fixture on trains but a few club cars were thus equipped. Many railroads had passengers or railroad workers who could play piano. If no one else was available, Josh himself would play. He was self-taught and played the instrument reasonably well. But it was not his playing that enthralled the passengers as much as his powerful voice. Josh would sing show tunes, gospel, and other popular tunes of southern origin. Josh had no great affection for these songs of the Old South, with their ingratiating lyrics of happy black people content with their status. But such performances always produced good tips so he at least was rewarded for their condescension. On rare occasions he would be accompanied by a passenger who happened to have his or her instrument on board. A regular passenger on the Richmond route would play his cornet. Another lady would sometimes accompany on her violin. When those impromptu concerts happened the ovation was enthusiastic and prolonged. Eventually Josh's talents grew in demand for birthdays, anniversaries and other special occasions. As a result, he soon found himself moving from one route to another as needed to keep up with the growing demand for his talent. On one memorable evening Josh and a small group of musicians actually were asked to perform in the terminal at Dallas for a special reception for the Governor of Texas. Josh delivered powerful versions of Texas anthems which roused the audience. Josh was on his way to a promising career.

All that changed on one unfortunate trip from Atlanta to Louisville. A lady from New Orleans seemed to have a great animosity for the black employees. Such passengers were usually easy to spot and Josh did his best, to the extent he was able, to avoid her. But the performance of his duties required him to serve her demands and she was haughty and condescending. Josh by now was very used to prejudice from passengers and could usually ignore it. Making matters worse the lady transported in her purse a flask from which she frequently imbibed. When she was drunk she went from merely rude to downright nasty. One terrible night she accused Josh of robbing her compartment of a family heirloom necklace she had worn on the trip. Silas Fletcher, the white conductor, took her side and immediately began a hostile interrogation of Josh in front of the lady who stood nearby smirking with bleary bloodshot eyes. At that point Fletcher initiated a search of the compartment where it was discovered the misplaced jewelry had simply fallen on the floor behind a suitcase. Clearing the matter conclusively the lady suddenly remembered she had been wearing the piece when she left the club car after dinner. Josh had been performing in the club car at that time so could not have been involved. Freed from suspicion, Josh at least expected an apology from Fletcher, if not from his accuser. Instead he received a stern warning that he would be watched closely from now on. That settled the matter for Josh. He did not expect Detroit to be perfect, but it had to be better than the South. From now on he would devote all his energy to getting to the Motor City. Whether he was fated to grace the boards of the Detroit Opera or merely turn a wrench as an anonymous laborer on an assembly line he would have the dignity and respect denied his people for so long.

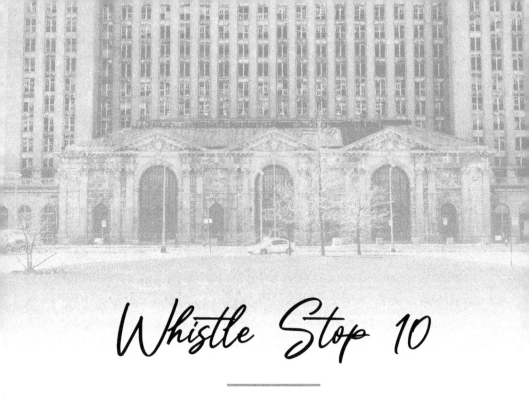

Whistle Stop 10

THE 1943 RIOT (PART 2)
GEORGE 1936-1941

The Super Chief from Cincinnati arrived at Michigan Central at 4:30 PM on a beautiful Saturday afternoon in early spring. On board was Josh Holloway. He had been riding the rails now for seven months, biding his time and drawing every nearer to his final destination in Detroit. His growing notoriety as a performer had greatly facilitated his ability to choose the trains on which he worked. All of the rail lines were interested in hiring him so Josh had accomplished something that very few blacks in the era of Jim Crow were able to do. He had a measure of control over his employment and was able to pick and choose where he worked. He had used this freedom to eventually secure employment on the Illinois-Ohio railroad which served Toledo and Detroit. Today he arrived for the first time in Detroit where he anticipated a reunion with his uncle George, his father Cyrus's brother. Josh had been enticed to come to Detroit by the promise of a good paying factory job, but he was already having second thoughts. He knew that he would never find fulfillment in the mind numbing regimentation of factory life. His career goal, he now knew, was to become a professional singer. He knew that the Detroit Metropolitan Opera was highly regarded and he dreamed of one day performing there. Lingering in the back of his mind was the fear he might not be able to make it in the classical operatic theatre. He could not speak Italian or German which he knew were the languages of the opera. He had listened to the recordings of famous arias and would sing them but always felt insecure with words he did not understand and could not pronounce. But he also knew there were abundant jazz clubs in the city where he might get jobs. So one way or the other he hoped to use his voice to make a living. In the meantime while he waited for an opportunity to present itself, he would continue his employment with the railroad. That provided him a secure income while continuing to improve his vocal styling. He could work exclusively in the Northeast corridor and not set foot in the South, the bigotry of Jim Crow left behind with its economic and cultural bondage.

Josh believed he had finally reached sanctuary in Detroit. Once the last stop along the Underground Railroad for fugitive slaves on their way to Canada, the city now offered the hope of a new life for Joshua Holloway. What Josh did not know in the euphoria of his arrival was that the Ku Klux Klan in the 1920s and early 30s had one of its largest memberships in the north in Michigan. It's direct descendent, the violent Black Legion, had terrorized minority communities in the city as recently as the early 1930s. Even here in the north the country was not inoculated against the infection of racism. Josh had not escaped entirely.

Josh's first glimpse of the city was through the window of the club car as the train slowly decelerated entering the terminal. He could hardly contain his excitement. He had seen every major railroad station in the South, from Dallas to Atlanta. Detroit's station, at first glance, seemed much the same; impressive, monumental style with classical touches, asserting prosperity and modernity; an inviting nexus for countless people on the move. Railroad stations in the South seemed determined to project a return to normalcy after the devastation of the civil war. The country had changed in many ways since that bitter conflict. The old boundaries between North and South were obliterated from the map. Removing them from the nation's heart would take longer. The division between the regions now was rooted mostly in the Souths deep lingering resentment over their defeat and reconstruction. The shame over the lingering stain of slavery was more or less forgotten. To rationalize this, historians and politicians in the south advanced their subtle but insidious theory of the Lost Cause. Slavery was minimized or overlooked entirely as a cause of the conflict. According to this doctrine the civil war was merely an inevitable struggle over the issue of States Rights and regional self-determination. Slavery was footnoted as only one minor aspect of the conflict; hard money, tariffs, trade, life style, and congressional representation; being the more consequential causes. The war was cultural and economic but not moral. This permitted a degree of Southern justification over their catastrophic defeat. This mood was tragically manifested in Jim Crow legislation throughout the south restoring the de-facto antebellum way of life. This was the world from which Josh sought escape.

Josh found Uncle George on the platform waiting for him. The two men embraced warmly. George had been sojourning in this northern city for nearly five years and this was his first reunion with his kin. Naturally George was hungry for all the news from home and those remaining in Mississippi. It was an emotional meeting for the two. George had prepared in advance his small house in the nearby Black Bottom neighborhood to accommodate his nephew. The neighborhood had become recently the destination of hundreds of black migrants from the South that had, like Josh, come north to seek a better life. The term "Black Bottom" was historically a description of the rich soil in the area along the riverbank, the best farmland in the region. Only recently the term had come to mean something else.

In the ensuing weeks Josh got the lay of the land. The Black Bottom neighborhood was just a short bus ride from Michigan Central. The housing in the neighborhood was generally run down with too many residents and too little room. George did his best to maintain his property but it was sorely in need of paint and windows. Uncle George had an old beat up truck that he drove to work daily at the Ford Rouge plant. Josh was frequently away on the railroad so the two did not often get in each other's way. George was a quiet church going man who attended the Ebenezer AME church only a block away from his residence. From living alone he had become a good cook and made most of the meals the two shared. The housemates fell into an easy companionable relationship. Josh felt he could continue this comfortable life indefinitely but he knew this could not go on forever. He was determined to pursue his career ambition. It was also about time he found himself a wife.

Crossing Gratiot Avenue to the north of Black Bottom was found the bustling district of Paradise Valley. Here hundreds of black owned businesses thrived. It was this community within the city that provided all of the necessities for the Black Bottom community. Everything from retail to grocery stores, banks, barbershops, doctors, dentists and beauty parlors, could be found here. It was also the center of a rich and varied night life with interesting restaurants serving delicious food, night clubs, theatres, and of greatest interest to Josh, numerous jazz clubs. Much like the larger and better known black enclaves of Harlem in New York, Deep Ellum in Dallas, Underground Atlanta, and the Southside of Chicago, this area attracted crowds of white residents seeking out its many pleasures. Along Hastings Street many of the clubs were clustered: Jake's, the Paradise Theatre, The Tropicana, Club Harlem, The Horseshoe Bar, Flame Show Bar, and Sportees Lounge. These venues attracted top talent from around the country. Artists like Fats Waller, Count Basie, Cab Calloway, Bojangles

Robinson, Duke Ellington, Billie Holiday and Ella Fitzgerald; all frequently performed at Paradise Valley hot spots. Josh Holloway was in good company but would have to be lucky to make his own name among such a constellation of stars. On nights when he was in town Josh would walk the streets enjoying the background of delicious aromas from the restaurants and wonderful music overflowing the night clubs and pouring into the street. He wanted to be a part of this.

Early in 1940, George got terrible news from his brother Cyrus. His beloved Harriet, Josh's mother, had passed away from a bout with the flu the month before. This was followed only three weeks later by the passing of Mr. Emmitt Prejean. All of the lands he owned were to be auctioned off and Cyrus was told he would have to vacate the property. The girls Maya and Lulu were both married now and seemed to be doing well. Maya the youngest was a domestic for a kind white family and Lulu was a teacher in Mound Bayou. Cyrus suggested Clem join his father in Detroit since he no longer had employment in Mississippi. Cyrus for his part would remain in Bolivar County because he could not bear to leave his daughters and the sacred plot of earth occupied by his beloved wife. With no family to provide for, Cyrus was confident he could scratch out a living hiring his labor in Mound Bayou. George and Josh were both deeply saddened by the news. Relieving their grief was the prospect of reunion with Clem. George immediately wrote back and the arrangements were made. The tiny house in Black Bottom was to add another occupant.

Clem found employment with his father working on the Ford assembly line and in a short time seemed to adapt to his new environment. He like his father faced the workplace prejudice common to the factory but mostly ignored it. The cold weather was the worst trial for him, but mercifully that first winter was uncharacteristically mild giving him a chance to ease into the harsher climate. In time he met a cleaning lady employed in the downtown Hudson's department store with whom he started to keep company. The two of them seemed destined to be married. Josh, for his part, was starting to make some contacts in the entertainment field and occasionally performed at some of the clubs in Paradise Valley. Their comfortable way of life was about to be upended by two unforeseen circumstances, the outbreak of war, and the entrance of a woman into Josh Holloways life.

In spring of 1941, Josh found occasional jobs in the Harlem Club, not as a headliner but a fill in when needed. The managers of the club liked him well enough but thought his voice wasn't quite bluesy enough for the jazz scene. A little too operatic. Josh found himself stuck in the middle artistically. His sober lifestyle was also at odds with his fellow musicians. He openly disdained the marijuana and cocaine use common among jazz club musicians. He had promised his mother when he left Mississippi he would never give in to the temptations of alcohol and big city vices. Josh was determined to live clean to fulfill the promise he made. He also did not want to repay the kindness of his religious uncle who had taken him in, with bad behavior. But it made him a bit of a misfit for the club life. He still had his railroad job but he knew it was time to confront the obstacles and take the plunge. God gave him a voice for a reason and he had to find the best way to use it. Giving up security for a shot at his true ambition was scary but Josh knew if he did not do it soon, he might not ever.

In the summer of 1941 Josh met Pearl Blanchette, a chorus girl at the Harlem Club where he had landed a temporary gig. One Friday evening, after his set, Josh watched the chorus girls perform from the wing of the stage. He noticed the pretty leggy dancer in the front row immediately and determined to meet her. After summoning his nerve Josh approached the girl and asked her for a late night date after her last show. They strolled to a nearby diner open 24 hours. Workers from the assembly plants would frequently eat here after their shift and the place was crowded even at this late hour. The two shared a club breakfast, fried chicken and waffles. They found they had much in common. She was twenty and a recent arrival from Tennessee accompanying her family looking for work in the automobile industry. She was determined to become a nurse. She used her talent and love of dancing to find temporary employment in the clubs of Paradise Valley. She admitted it was hard to discourage all the unwanted advances of the musicians and occasionally customers. But the word soon got out that she was not a party girl and the unwelcome attention diminished. Quiet and studious she went about her business on stage but avoided the parties the rest of the girls frequented. Her strict parents disapproved of this employment but relented after discovering she made more than enough money for tuition and books at Wayne State University. They still disliked the club scene, but eventually came around. In the end they trusted her to do the right thing. The friendship between Josh and Pearl blossomed over time and the two seemed certain to marry as soon as Josh could find the right spot in the local music scene. He had decided to finish out the year on the railroad and begin his new life in 1942. His last scheduled run in December would take him to New York and Buffalo.

December 7th, 1941

Magda and Bella Moskowitz, twin sisters and fellow graduates of the Julliard School in New York were enroute to Detroit to perform with the DSO as guest musicians. Bella was a violinist and Magda a cellist. They were the daughters of Leopold, a college professor of the humanities. They had fled their native Budapest shortly after the Nazis came to power in Germany. The anti-Semitic pogroms growing throughout Europe had turned increasingly violent. Leo had several cousins and a brother already living in the United States who for years had urged him to escape while he was able. It was the violence of Kristallnacht in 1938 that convinced him Jews were simply not safe in Europe any longer. The Moskowitz family made it out just in time.

The sisters occupied a sleeper compartment on the overnight train from New York. They did not wish to be separated from their instruments, not trusting them to handling and storage in the baggage car. The two cases took up considerable space in the cramped compartment. Bella, after exhausting all efforts to pass the time observing the passing scenery outside her window took out her violin and began to play. Magda soon joined in and the two musicians began to rehearse one of their selections for their performance in Detroit, a lively Mozart duet. It was midmorning on a quite Sunday and the car was barely half full. Soon the air was filled with sublime music. Passengers on their way to lunch in the club car gathered outside the door of their compartment enraptured by the glorious sounds. At length Josh Holloway arrived on the scene. He stood largely ignored at the rear of the gathered passengers. He listened intently, savoring each note. The ovation when the sisters finished was enthusiastic and they were implored to continue. The women after a moment of thought offered a piece they felt appropriate for a Sunday morning. Josh knew the song well having sung it at funerals at Brother Franklin's church in Mound Bayou. He raised his voice in accompaniment to the strings.

> "Nearer My God to Thee, nearer to Thee!
> E'en though it be a cross that raiseth me
> Still all my song shall be…
> Nearer My God to Thee
> Nearer my God to Thee, nearer to Thee!"

When the last notes of the hymn faded several of the listeners wiped tears from their faces clearly moved by the moment. The sisters were equally affected and each in turn embraced Josh sharing the intimacy only creators of transcendent beauty can experience. Josh chatted with the ladies and assured them he would be on hand to assist them upon their arrival in Detroit. The ladies were confident he would take excellent care of their instruments and agreed gratefully.

Upon their arrival at Michigan Central in the late afternoon it was clear that something was happening. There were the crowds appropriate for that hour but absent was the bustle of people hurrying to board trains. It almost seemed as if people had stopped mid-stride, frozen into untimely poses. As Josh and the Moskowitz sisters advanced through the terminal they soon learned the reason why. The crowds were clustered under a loud speaker broadcasting momentous news. Josh heard the words: "Pearl Harbor", "Japan", "sneak attack" and knew immediately what had happened. The voice over the loudspeaker described heavy losses and near destruction of the Pacific fleet. The three musicians were momentarily stunned. All the important things going on in their lives, all the prejudice each had encountered and the dangers they had faced, all their artistic aspirations; all seemed to disappear in one moment of paralyzing uncertainty. Once the three caught their breath it was as if they were simultaneously seized by the same inspiration. In this moment of profound tragedy music was the most eloquent statement they could offer. They conferred briefly on their selections. The sisters removed their instruments from their cases and began to play. Josh Holloway stood in the center between the pair and began to sing:

> "My county tis of thee,
> Sweet land of Liberty
> Of thee I sing,
> Land where my fathers died
> Land of the Pilgrim's pride
> From every mountainside
> Let freedom ring."

For the next half hour the trio offered hymns and patriotic songs. The crowd gathering in front of them listened reverently as if attending a Church service. The three artists, two Jewish women and a black man, unappreciated refugees in their own country, offered a concert full of hope and resolution. Both of these would be sorely needed in the days to come.

Whistle Stop 11

THE 1943 RIOT (PART 3)
CLEM 1942-1943

Although Josh Holloway no longer rode the rails as on employee of the railroads, he still frequently boarded the bus in his Black Bottom neighborhood for the short ride to the Michigan Central Station. There he worked at the USO lounge seeing to the comfort and entertainment of traveling servicemen on their way to or from the war. He worked in the cantina passing out sandwiches and coffee and a song or two while the servicemen waited for their trains. This work was not indispensable to the war effort and did not magnify his fame or honor, but Josh felt in a small way he was helping out. He had been medically disqualified from joining the service himself due to a condition he did not even know he had. As a young man the chronic foot pain that bothered him was attributed to his long hours behind the plow. As a porter he found that being on his feet all day caused him discomfort, but no suspicion of anything majorly wrong, even though the pain frequently made him limp. It was only after taking his military medical exam that the problem was identified. It was an abnormality of his arches commonly called flat feet. It was understood that long hours of marching would not be possible. This was a disqualifying condition for a potential soldier but not for an entertainer. So he devoted his services to the USO while working the club circuit in Paradise Valley when he could get jobs. With the war on he was doubtful a big break would soon come his way. His cousin Clem was also exempted from the draft because of his job in wartime industrial production. The Holloway's contribution to the war effort would be stateside. The little house in Black Bottom would still be crowded with three residents.

The principal advantage of not being drafted for both Josh and Clem was they did not have to separate from their girlfriends. Josh and Pearl were determined to be married soon as were Clem and Althea Blaine, the woman from Hudson's department store. Like all romances in wartime, there was a certain urgency to get on with it, a desire to seize the moment since the future was so uncertain. Even though it appeared the two cousins would be spared being called up, they still felt the pressure to tie the knot as quickly as possible. Many an innocent girl had been rushed to bed, if not the altar, to solidify a relationship that might not survive the war.

On one Friday afternoon in late February, Josh was performing his duties at the USO lounge in Michigan Central for the usual crowd of servicemen. The sandwiches having been distributed Josh sat at the piano and began his concert. The old standard: "I'll be seeing you" started off his set. He received a warm response from the audience. He performed several more tunes as soldiers arrived and left as their trains were called. At the end of his set he was approached by a staff Sargent who introduced himself as Richard Meyer. He explained that he was a cousin of Cheryl Crawford. The name did not register with Josh and he delivered a polite but blank facial expression. Meyer explained his cousin was a Broadway producer who had recently opened a revival of the Gershwin Opera *Porgy and Bess* at the Majestic Theatre in New York. The production had been running for a month to generally good reviews. The vocalist playing Porgy was the baritone Todd Duncan, a well-regarded artist Josh knew of by reputation. Meyer went on to explain the success of the show required them to hire additional performers for understudy roles and Meyer suggested he could arrange an audition right here in Detroit if Josh was interested. Opportunity had come calling for Joshua Holloway. Meyer made the arrangements at a pay phone nearby. The audition would take place in a week at the Tropicana, a club Josh knew well and where he had occasionally performed. Representatives from the show would hear him sing.

Early in March, Josh found himself on a train bound for New York. Pearl had been ambivalent about this unexpected development. She was excited but also a bit dismayed this would delay their wedding. Josh assured her if he was successful and this became a long term job, he would send for her and they could be married in New York. She was very busy completing her studies at Wayne State and would earn her degree by the end of summer. The temporary separation might actually prove beneficial. In the end the opportunity was too good to pass on and Pearl had tearfully seen him off at the station. As the miles of scenery passed beyond his window Josh had lots of time to think. He was filled with powerful emotions he could barely contain. It seemed a lifetime ago he plowed the Mississippi bottom land where his only audience was an ornery old mule. Strange fate indeed. He thought about the prosperity that was sure to come his way. Now there would be nothing to prevent him and Pearl getting married. He thought of Cyrus and his sisters still in Mississippi. How proud they must feel over his success. Mostly he thought about the future, now suddenly bright and full of promise.

Josh Holloway appeared in 49 performances of *Porgy and Bess*, understudying both characters of Porgy and his antagonist Crown, while on most nights a member of the chorus. He enjoyed both leading roles but liked playing the villain Crown a little more. He received positive reviews from the newspapers. These he clipped from the pages of the New York Times and mailed back to the family in Detroit and Mississippi along with the money he had earned beyond his living expenses. He received good news from his family in reply. Pearl had finished her degree and now was a college graduate, soon to be a registered nurse. Josh was so proud he could not resist boasting to all the cast at the Majestic who congratulated him heartily. The other momentous news was Cousin Clem and Althea were expecting a baby. The couple was terribly excited and George was ecstatic to welcome his first grandchild. They quickly married in a civil ceremony. While Josh was upset not to have been there for the wedding he understood the situation and quickly got over his disappointment. What an eventful year 1942 was turning out to be. 1943 was sure to be amazing.

The New York run of *Porgy and Bess* came to an end in September. The cast had a party at the Cotton Club in Harlem to celebrate the show's success. There was just a tinge of the usual sadness when a show closes. But it was soon turned to joy with the announcement the show was being taken on tour and the entire cast was being retained. One of its first stops was the Cass Theatre in Detroit. Josh Holloway's career carousel was spinning him home to Pearl.

Even as Josh contemplated this happy turn of events there were momentous changes underway in Detroit that would soon engulf all the Holloways. The economic boom resulting from the conversion of automotive manufacturing to war-time production attracted droves of black immigrants from the south hoping to secure steady work and a dependable income working in war production. While the labor was needed, there was simply no place for all these migrants to live. Low cost housing in neighborhoods like Black Bottom was substandard when it could be found at all. The result was dangerous overcrowding in neighborhoods that were already poor and struggling to stay afloat. The black laborers had few alternatives as they could neither afford nor were welcome in more desirable neighborhoods. Municipal services like sanitation and the fire department deteriorated rapidly in these crowded neighborhoods making them more unsafe. Drug and alcohol abuse increased. Schools for the worker's children were overcrowded and substandard. These conditions were ripe for eruptions of crime and violence. When unrest did breakout it was confronted by a mostly white police force that seemed more interested in restoring order by force than protecting the community. Charges of police brutality were increasing but seldom prosecuted.

The most impactful aspect of this increasing tension was now being displayed in the workplace. As part of the War Production Act, President Roosevelt insisted on ending racial discrimination in the factories in an effort to quickly maximize production. This policy, well intentioned as it was, did not stop racial tension from infecting the workplace. Blacks were always given the most menial, back breaking and dangerous jobs in the factory, often in the foundries where the work with molten metal risked ghastly industrial accidents and constant respiratory distress. There were virtually no black supervisors anywhere within the factory nor opportunities for black workers to earn better paid, higher skilled jobs. George Holloway could tell first hand that things were getting worse. When he first started working at the plant he had found racism to be frustrating but manageable. He kept to himself and was mostly tolerated by his white co-workers. Now, as the number of black workers increased bitter harassment led to frequent confrontations on the shop floor. Naturally this was blamed on black malcontents. Conditions were rapidly heading toward a dangerous explosion.

Clem and Althea welcomed a son, Jackson, to the world in late 1942. The new family crowded into the small house owned by George. It was tight but they were getting by. With any luck they would be able to find a place of their own in time. The government had been actively building affordable housing to alleviate the shortage. In 1941 the Sojourner Truth housing project was opened in what the government hoped was a good location, at the intersection of Nevada and Fenelon streets. This was already a low income neighborhood and it was intended to provide residency for primarily black citizens. Not unexpectedly, white residents of nearby neighborhoods demanded the project be reserved for white occupancy only. The municipal and federal governments acceded to this pressure and attempted to find an alternative location for the black community. When such a location could not be found, tension to integrate Sojourner Truth erupted into dozens of protests throughout the city. In the end, integration of the complex succeeded but resentment in both communities seethed. This was the highly combustible state of affairs that Josh faced when he returned from New York. It would be impossible for George, Josh's, and Clem's growing families; to fit into a single house. Josh would simply have to find a place of his own. He was better equipped to do that since he still had much of the money he earned in *Porgy and Bess*.

Josh was able to find residence in Paradise Valley a few blocks off Hastings Avenue with easy access to all the night clubs in the area. He and Pearl were married shortly thereafter. Josh had decided not to continue on tour with Porgy after it left Detroit since that would require separations from his family. Besides, he now knew that he wanted to open a club of his own where he could perform but still go home at night to his wife. A suitable vacant movie theatre was available and a lease was signed. A liquor license was secured and renovations on the property began. In April of 1943, "Holloways Oasis" opened. It soon was being called "The Hollow" by Paradise Valley residents. Its owner and featured performer, fresh from his success in the Broadway revival of Porgy and Bess was Joshua Holloway. Despite the war, business was very good. War time production ran mostly three shifts a day, seven days a week, turning out all the implements of modern warfare. There were always workers from the latest shift seeking a bit of entertainment and relaxation after work. Restaurants, movie theaters, and the Hollow stayed open long hours to accommodate them. This too, was Josh's contribution to the war effort.

June 21, 1943

It was a lovely summer day. A little hot for this time of year, but still perfect picnic weather. Crowds of people were enjoying the view of the city skyline from Belle Isle in the middle of the Detroit River. Life in wartime was stressful but for the most part everyone was optimistic and the community settled in a comfortable routine of long hours of work and deeply prized leisure. Families with soldiers in Europe or the Pacific still faced the constant dread of bad news; but for those fortunate ones, not separated from their loved ones by the war, life was good. Business was booming and the community seemed of one mind content to take the day off and enjoy the nice weather with their families. Among their number were Clem, Althea and baby Jackson. Clem had a ukulele which he played with enthusiasm if not great skill. He knew that Josh had all the musical talent in the family but he was not envious. Althea accompanied on harmonica: "You are my sunshine, my only sunshine"… Jackson laughed happily, before drifting off to sleep on the blanket spread out on the grass. Clem and Althea dozed in the humid shade of an oak. Suddenly the peacefulness of the afternoon was shattered by the sound of angry shouting. Swarms of people, black and white, began racing toward the Belle Island Bridge, the sole exit from the island. Clem could see there was a brawl underway with numerous white teenagers attacking a group of black youth. From that distance it was impossible to tell who started the fighting but Clem knew he must lead his family to safety and quickly. Althea grabbed the baby while Clem scooped up the blanket and basket and ran for the bridge. They were halfway across when suddenly the fighting broke out all around them. There were fistfights and rock throwing completely encircling them. Five white youths surrounded them and cut off their escape. Clem raised his ukulele like a club and began swinging it in wide arcs trying to defend his family. The circle of attackers closed in. One brandished a baseball bat which he swung wildly and caught Clem full on the back of his neck. He fell unconscious on the bridge. Althea looked on in horror, screaming in agony while shielding her baby from the assailants. The sound of approaching police caused the attackers to flee the scene in the direction of the city. The police administered first aid to Clem who was bleeding from his mouth and ears. He was gathered up and dispatched by ambulance to the closest hospital with Althea and Jackson riding stunned and weeping hysterically alongside.

Clem Holloway, 27, father of one, was the first fatality of the 1943 Detroit Race Riot. For the extended Holloway family it was an unimaginable tragedy. The riot continued to swirl around the city for two more days but the family was oblivious to the ongoing violence so numb with pain they were. The white gang that had started the brawl eventually carried the conflict into the black neighborhoods roughing up anyone they could grab. The mayor and governor petitioned President Roosevelt who quickly dispatched federal troops to the city to restore order.

Lessening the grief of the family only slightly, was the arrival of Julius Cyrus Holloway, first born son of Josh and Pearl, born just two weeks before the day the riots broke out. Josh's joy and optimism at the birth of a son had been dashed by the loss of Clem. His joy had turned to despair with stunning swiftness. From now on he would grip his wife and baby son with new urgency, desperate to keep them safe from harm forever.

The final death count for the riot would exceed 30, of which most were black. An "official" investigation afterwards, not surprisingly, lay most of the blame on the black community. This despite the fact the white rioters greatly outnumbered the black. Also the profile of the white insurgents was younger, unemployed, and having traveled great distance within the city, to participate in the violence. By comparison, blacks involved in the riot were fewer, generally older and employed, and defending themselves in their own neighborhood.

A week after the riots had ended, Josh held a memorial service at the Hollow for Clem and all the other members of the community killed in the violence. It was a heartbreaking occasion with scores of family friends all crowded into the club paying respects and sharing grief. Cyrus Holloway and his pastor Brother Franklin had made the long trip from Mississippi with tickets purchased by Josh and George. Only the girls, Lulu and Maya very busy with new-born of their own, could not get away and were absent. Josh had let a choir in moving collection of hymns in tribute to all the fallen. Brother Franklin gave an emotional eulogy which assured the congregation that Clem was enjoying his eternal reward. He pleaded eloquently for reconciliation and forgiveness as the best way to carry on in his memory. Sadly that message was only delivered to half of the community that needed to hear it. Burial followed after in the historic Woodlawn Cemetery west of Woodward Avenue. All the family and friends returned to the Hollow for an early dinner provided by the ladies of the AME church community. But Josh had one stop to make before he rejoined his family.

After a short bus ride, he found himself strolling on the Belle Isle Bridge, now rinsed clean of its stain, overlooking the slow moving current. Though the residue of violence was washed away by the river's flow, the terrible memorial would always stand. The river had carried its tint of innocent blood to mix in the basin of the sea. Submerged in those depths were regretful tears, contrition and atonement for all the past sins of humankind. Josh came to offer one last farewell to his fallen cousin.

> "Old Man River, that Old Man River
> He don't say nothin but must know somethin
> But Old Man River
> He just keeps rolling along…."

He had sung these words hundreds of times but their meaning had never been clearer. Life was hard and there was no way to change that. Whether you understood your destiny or had no idea why you were here, didn't really matter, life keeps rolling along, revealing its long, slow purpose over its course. He felt the currents in his own life carrying him as he drifted on through all the pain and uncertainty. The last verse of the hymn was a poignant expression of acute pain felt by so many of his people.

"I gets weary and sick of trying
I'm tired of living but scared of dying
But Old Man river, he jes keeps rollin along"

As he slowly retreated from the bridge he thought of Jackson and Julius. It would be up to them to carry on. They must build the better world their fathers had imagined but failed to reach.

Whistle Stop 12

AUGUST 3, 1937

The Churchmen

There was great excitement in Michigan Central Station portending an event of great importance. Citizens of Detroit were well accustomed to the arrival of celebrities in the Midwestern Metropolis, but one arriving today on the 7:19 PM from Rochester, New York was a figure of unusual significance. By 4:00 PM thousands had already gathered in the waiting rooms of the station while many more congregated in the green expanse of Roosevelt Park just outside. All were gathered to see and welcome the arrival of Edward Mooney, the leader of the newly established Archdiocese of Detroit. Already renowned as an industrial powerhouse, the city would now be a spiritual epicenter for nearly a million Roman Catholics. Archbishop Mooney would become at once, a pastor to his disparate flock and a political figure of considerable influence.

It was this duality of secular power and religious devotion that had strongly shaped the city from its very beginning in 1701. The party of French Canadians under the leadership of Antoin de Cadillac landed at the point of land they named Fort Pontchartrain du Detroit on July 24. They immediately began to clear the land for the construction of a stockade in the wilderness. Significantly, it was only two days later that the settlers began construction of a chapel dedicated to St. Anne, the mother of Mary, and grandmother of Jesus, whose feast day the Church celebrated on that day. The original chapel was the first building completed in Detroit. Now 185 years after the founding of the city the latest considerably more magnificent, church building resided only a few blocks from Michigan Central Station where excited crowds were gathering to welcome the new Archbishop. Detroit had become, by 1937, a bastion of factories and faith. Nearly every immigrant who labored tirelessly in the mills and factories all week long gathered in their respective parish church communities on Sunday. The Poles, Irish, Italians, Germans, Greeks and Hungarians, all built their own churches frequently only separated by a few city blocks. Such is the enduring power of faith refracted through the prism of nationality. These impressive churches projected skyward over the collection of mostly low residential buildings that surrounded them and whose spiritual welfare they oversaw. Their tall spires and steeples suggested islands protruding from the flat surface of the ocean. In the end, however, it was not this polyglot collection of congregations, but the strength of its industrial might that won the city its rank as an Archdiocese. Over 100 other municipalities were considered for this status but in the end it was Detroit's impressive muscle that decided the matter. The hard times of the Great Depression lingered and prosperity remained elusive. Despite that, Detroit was still a model of American ingenuity and productivity and the Holy

See could not help but notice. When recovery finally did occur, Detroit was going to play an important role in getting people back on their feet. In those times, as in our own, the Church resides in that thin separation between the here and the hereafter, ushering souls from one world to the next, with feet planted firmly in either domain. Archbishop Mooney had his work cut out for him. He would have to deftly balance the concerns of both sides of the divide.

Over all, the shadow of economic uncertainty still remained. It had been five years since President Roosevelt had begun the sweeping New Deal, whose force and reach had begun to reshape American politics and society. Not surprisingly, his agenda had sparked controversy along predictably political fault lines, those who desired an activist government with its promised social safety net; and those for whom this all smacked of socialism and bitterly opposed it. Among those opposed was the very powerful Detroiter Henry Ford, whose unyielding anti-union stance and thinly veiled anti-Semitism would eventually provoke violence. Overarching all this national tension were the ever more ominous rumblings of unrest in Europe and the rise of National Socialism in Germany. It was within this moment of economic and political ferment that Archbishop Mooney arrived in Detroit to begin his reign.

The train carrying the new Archbishop stopped briefly in Windsor to pick up some of the clerical dignitaries that would officiate over the installation ceremonies. Included in this group was the delegation from the Vatican. Proceeding through the Windsor Tunnel they arrived in Michigan Central to be greeted by the Governor of Michigan and the Mayor of the city. After exiting the train, the party processed down a long facing double line of ceremonially clad Knights of Columbus, resplendent in their traditional regalia, their raised crossed swords forming a canopy of steel blades. The waiting room was festooned with welcoming banners many proudly displaying shamrocks hung by the residents of nearby Corktown, to honor their fellow Irishman. The party proceeded outside the terminal to a raised platform at the head of Roosevelt Park, by now thronged with a crowd estimated at between 50 and 100 thousand of the faithful and the merely curious. A black vocalist dressed in the distinctive livery of a Pullman porter, opened the ceremony with a stirring rendition of Schubert's Ave Maria, which the crowd received warmly. The welcoming remarks by the church, municipal, and state delegations preceded the new Archbishop's address to the crowd. One of the speakers; James Fitzgerald, delivered remarks on behalf of the laity. He spoke glowingly on the absence of bigotry and the commitment to tolerance in the community that Mooney was now called to lead. This sentiment sadly, was more aspirational than literal which would be made clear in the coming years. As long as the old foes of humanity greed and want endured-the work of the Church would remain incomplete. Fitzgerald concluded his oration:

"We welcome you to this, now your city, your state, and
   your home.
You lead. We will follow. A million hearts are saying to
   you tonight:
Welcome and God bless you always."

Upon completion of the ceremonies the group traveled in motorcade to the apostolic residence in Palmer Park preceded by a squadron of police motorcycles. The installation ceremony itself was conducted in the neo Gothic cathedral of the Blessed Sacrament on Woodward Avenue the following morning. The ceremony had all the pomp and ritual of the medieval pageant from which it evolved over the centuries. Due to the seating limitations in the Church, the attendance was limited to local clergy and important delegations from around the country. One of those in attendance was a well-known priest from the nearby community of Royal Oak. His name was Charles Coughlin and he would be the object of the new Archbishop's attention in coming weeks.

Charles Edward Coughlin was Canadian born to a strict Irish Catholic family. He was ordained to the priesthood in Toronto and came to Detroit by way of Windsor in 1923. By 1926 he had become a media figure with a weekly broadcast over the airwaves of WJR radio. His broadcast initially was low key, offering a talk format blend of cultural and religious views. He was an early and enthusiastic supporter of Franklin Roosevelt and heartily endorsed the New Deal. By the start of FDR's second term Coughlin's original support turned to opposition, largely because Coughlin resented not being given a more prominent voice in the Democratic administration. Coughlin felt he had helped Roosevelt get elected but now the President was trying to distance himself. Whether motivated by ideology or frustrated ambition his views became increasingly incendiary and bitterly critical of FDR. His broadcasts had devolved into weekly political diatribes not even remotely religious in nature. Church and government officials would eventually try to stifle his recalcitrant voice by limiting first amendment protection of the airwaves and disallowance of the post office from distributing politically charged material. These tactics proved legally problematic and unable to suppress Coughlin, whose influence continued to grow. At his peak of power he received on average over 80,000 pieces of mail weekly and boasted tens of millions of listeners to his radio program. The post office in Royal Oak had to be enlarged just to manage the weekly avalanche of letters.

Archbishop Mooney was aware of Coughlin prior to his arrival in Detroit. While still in serving in Rochester, New York, Mooney received a letter from Father John Burke, an official of a prominent Catholic organization. The letter recounted how Coughlin had roundly condemned Roosevelt at a political convention, calling him a liar and a betrayer for failure to reform the monetary system. As a final gesture of defiance, as if to emphasize his disgust, Coughlin reached for his throat and ripped off his priestly collar.

All this was bad enough but even more troubling was Coughlin's increasingly venomous exhortations of Anti-Semitism. After the shocking carnage of Kristallnacht in Germany with its terrible destruction of Jewish lives and property, Coughlin suggested the rampage was justified.

He blamed the Jews for starting the persecution and they were simply getting what they deserved. On another occasion he issued perhaps his most inflammatory pronouncement to a political gathering in the Bronx. He raised his arm in the Nazi salute and thundered:

"When we get through with the Jews in America, they'll think the treatment they received in Germany was nothing."

Such reprehensible speech made Coughlin a hero of fascist Germany and Italy. Within those two nations his every utterance was widely distributed and powerful propaganda for Hitler and Mussolini. But it was the outspoken criticism of FDR'S appointment of Hugo Black to the Supreme Court that inspired some of Coughlin's fiercest denunciations. He accused FDR of being insane over this selection. Black, a southerner, was a figure of some controversy with suspected ties to the Klan. But FDR admired his progressive initiative on behalf of the New Deal. His attacks renewed the ire of both the government and church leaders who seemed once again undecided how to silence his voice.

It fell to Mooney to stifle Coughlin for good. The relationship between the two men had been contentious since the beginning. Finally something had to be done. Under threat of federal charges of sedition brought against Coughlin, Mooney had no choice and acted decisively. He ordered Coughlin to cease all his political activity and confine his priestly ministry to a parish community. This was demanded as a nonnegotiable condition for remaining a priest. As Mooney diplomatically described the rebuke later:

"My understanding with him (Coughlin) is sufficiently broad and firm to exclude effectively the recurrence of any such unpleasant situation(s)"

Coughlin complied with his orders and quietly assumed his pastoral duties as the rector of the Shrine of the Little Flower in Royal Oak Michigan. There he served dutifully until his retirement in 1966. He died in 1979 and was interred in the Holy Sepulcher Cemetery in Southfield Michigan. His controversial life story remains significant footnote in a tumultuous era of American history.

For Mooney, his ministry through the war years saw tremendous growth of the Church in Detroit and Oakland County. He was elevated to the rank of Cardinal in 1946. His journey to Rome to receive the Red Hat signifying a prince of the Church began at Michigan Central Station where he departed for New York, with a warm sendoff from a large crowd. The transatlantic fight to Italy was so unnerving that he resolved never to subject himself to the trauma of air travel again. Mooney delivered the benediction at the second inauguration of President Eisenhower. Several months later he was summoned to Rome again to attend the conclave following the death of Pope Pius XII. He was to be one of the first American born prelates to participate in the ancient ritual of papal conclave. This time he traveled more comfortably aboard a ship. As before, he started this, his final journey, at Michigan Central Station with an affectionate send-off reported by the Detroit Free Press. In his quarters in the Vatican just two hours before the start of Conclave, Cardinal Moony was stricken and died of a massive stroke. The earthly life of the first Archbishop of Detroit came to a close in the great center of Christendom only a short distance from the Papal chair he was charged to help fill. His untimely end when so close to fulfilling his historic responsibility was both a heart breaking irony and an appropriate ending for a beloved pastor. He was interred in Plymouth Michigan at St John's major seminary. In 1988 his remains were moved to the Holy Sepulcher Cemetery in Southfield Michigan where Charles Coughlin was laid to rest a decade earlier. Here these two significant Churchmen, despite their contention in life, found ultimate reconciliation in sacred ground. Rest in Peace.

Whistle Stop 13

APRIL 20, 1915

The Nurse

Madame Marie DePage would never neglect her appearance. Despite a grueling schedule of public appearances and the exertions of almost constant travel, she appeared fresh and charming to everyone she met. Her arrival in Detroit that Thursday was only one stop on a long journey to cities as far flung as San Francisco, Washington D.C and Pittsburgh. Unless you knew the purpose of her visit, you might suspect she was a wealthy matron on an extended holiday. She was in reality, a prominent humanitarian and nurse, on an urgent mission. She had been sent to the United States to raise funds for a desperately needed expansion of a hospital in her native Belgium. The Ocean Hotel had been quickly converted when the war broke out, from a resort, to a 200 bed hospital. After only a year of war, it was obvious that this was nowhere near enough beds. The appalling tide of war wounded was simply too overwhelming. The plan was to expand the property to accommodate 2000 beds. In war torn Europe, the funds for such a project were simply not available. So it was agreed that Marie would take her plea to America.

Marie was the wife of a prominent physician, Antoine DePage, the head of the Belgian Red Cross. Dr. DePage had founded the first medical school in Belgium and was a personal physician to Belgian nobility. He is credited as being the founder of the Doctors without Borders movement for his work in the Balkans several years before. Throughout all these far-reaching activities, Marie worked tirelessly at his side. Sometimes the work was dangerous. The political intrigue of the era placed her at constant risk. But she carried on her important work heedless of the threat. She was assisted by another nurse and dear friend, an Englishwoman named Edith Cavell.

When Marie stepped off the train in Michigan Central this morning she scanned the crowd for her welcoming delegation. She observed a tall, thin gentleman who approached her and introduced himself as Mr. Van Slembrouck, a local businessman and her assigned contact. He greeted her cordially and collected her bags. They exchanged pleasantries and agreed to go right to work. Van Slembrouck was to assist and coordinate the hospital appeal in Detroit.

There was a definite air of apprehension in the terminal this morning. The war news from Europe had people on edge. Most still believed that war on the continent was not America's business, and involvement should be avoided. President Wilson had echoed that sentiment. He had been elected the year before war broke out in Europe and had managed to maintain neutrality in his first term. He correctly read the nation's mood that this was not the New World's fight. Let the Old World battle it out. He was up for election again in another year and pinned his hopes on remaining neutral. Still, the public was wary of the German government's ominous warning in early 1915 of unlimited submarine warfare against all flagged vessels from belligerent nations. Within weeks that threat would be carried out. No one milling about in the station that morning, including Marie, had any inkling of the disaster about to overtake them.

Marie spent an exhausting two days in Detroit, spent in fund raising and public appearances. Her mission thus far had been successful and she was confidently anticipating her return to Belgium. Her departure from Michigan Central the next night, hurried her to the next stop of the tour. She would go on to raise over $100,000 from her American appeal, well in excess of her goal.

Shortly after, she received a wire alerting her that her youngest son Lucien had been called up and would be joining his older brother at the front. She urgently desired to return home as quickly as possible to see him off. She consulted the steam ship offices and was given a choice between two vessels bound for Europe. The ship *Lapland* would depart New York two days before the *Lusitania,* but being a slower vessel, would actually arrive in France on the same day as the faster *Lusitania.* She was aware of the German's announcement of unrestricted submarine warfare and the risk of sailing through the naval blockade. In the end, the deciding factor between the two was the desire to have two more days in America in support for her mission to raise critically needed funds. She purchased passage on the *Lusitania* for $142.50.

The choice would prove to be fatal. One of her traveling companions, Doctor James Houghton, mindful of the German threats, had made a new will the night before leaving New York. Marie dismissed his fears and described herself as a "happy fatalist". She retained her cautious optimism as the ship pulled from the dock on the start of its long voyage home to her family. While dreading her son's departure for the fighting she was at least buoyed by the success of her fund raising appeal. She thought of how happy and proud Antoine would be. She envisioned the hospital expansion, even as she prayed its extra beds would not ultimately be needed. She composed a letter to her dear friend and colleague Edith confiding all her feelings. Even though she could not post it until her arrival and Edith may well be there to meet her, she still poured out her feelings on paper. Next to her husband, Edith was her closest confidant. She was totally absorbed in her own thoughts and unaware of the menacing German U-boat that had been trailing them for hours. She like all the other passengers was taken by surprise by the explosion when the torpedo struck. Marie's nursing instincts instantly engaged. She was observed by several survivors of the sinking who recounted her bravery during her final hour. They saw her trying to assist children into lifeboats, and administering first aid to wounded passengers. At least one survivor saw her near the end, jumping from the awash portside deck. In that effort she became briefly entangled in ropes but managed to free herself just as the ship went down. Her body was later recovered and identified by her husband Antione. Marie's loss was a bitter blow to Edith Clavell, but Marie's dear friend would have little time to mourn her passing. In October of that year, Edith Clavell would be put on trial by a German military court for attempting to smuggle wounded Allied soldiers to safety in the neutral Netherlands. She was found guilty and executed by the Germans. When news of the heroic nurses spread, all of Belgium and England mourned.

The public outrage to the attack was instantaneous, but the anti-war sentiment in the United States was still strong. America would not join the war for another two years. The *Detroit Free Press* printed an article reporting Marie's death. It included speculation whether she was carrying the money she had raised on her US appeal when she died. Marie's grave was located just outside the hospital in Brussels where Antoine worked. It was placed where it could be seen from his office window. It was said for the rest of his life he would be seen frequently gazing out his window towards her gravestone.

Today in Brussels on the corner of Rue Marie DePage and Rue Edith Cavell is a bronze monument. Figures of a winged angel and a young lady are laying floral garlands on a granite tombstone. The inscription on the stone reads: "Passersby, Tell Your Children; How They Killed Them"

Whistle Stop 14

OCTOBER 15, 1923

The Tramp and the Secretary

Charlie's head bobbed as he fought against dozing off. A man of enormous energy it was difficult for him to sit idle for so long. If there was one thing he couldn't abide, it was boredom. At first the spectacle of magnificent scenery passing by the window of his Pullman car had captivated him. But as time passed his attention seemed to waver. For three days the train carrying him from the west coast had raced through all the varied landscapes of a diverse continent: breathtaking mountains, vast arid desert and the endless expanse of the great prairies. He was unaccustomed to so much space in this native England. He found it a little unnerving. Gradually his fertile mind turned from the monotonous grandeur of the view toward his next project. He began to anticipate his arrival in Detroit, his next stop on his cross country tour. He remembered his first visit to that Midwestern metropolis twelve years before. In 1911 he had been a part of a vaudevillian troupe on an extended three-year tour of America. Charlie had remembered the reception there as rather luke-warm and he himself had performed badly. One of his fellow troupers was another Englishman, Stan Laurel, who himself would achieve fame years later with his partner, Oliver Hardy. Stan used to tell the story how an unknown 22 year old had stood on the deck of the ship carrying them to America and predicted he would take the country by storm. "America, I am going to conquer you!" He bragged. "Every man, woman, and child shall have my name on their lips: Charles Spencer Chaplin!" he had prophesied. In the decade that followed Charlie made good his boast. He became the most famous actor and comedian in the country and in the process made himself enormously wealthy.

Charlie Chaplin got his big break while on that first American tour in 1913. In Philadelphia he got a telegram from Mack Sennett's Keystone Pictures. They were interested in hiring him to work in the fledgling motion picture business. Sennett had introduced the Keystone Cops to American audiences. His bumbling characters and chaotic pace enter-tained the public in the earliest days of silent pictures. Sennett had heard about Charlie Chaplin and offered him a contract for $150 a week, a princely sum in those days. Chaplin for his part was not convinced of the staying power of movies. He wrote his brother he intended to save as much as he could for five years and then retire from the business having achieved financial independence. He also predicted movies would prove to be a passing fad. After only a month into his contract, Charlie created the character for which he would become famous. He borrowed the pants of a heavy set Keystone actor, "Fatty Arbuckle" and coupled them with a too small coat from a much thinner man. He donned a Derby hat, a size too small. He completed the look with a small mustache to make him look older than his 24 years. He introduced the character to Mack Sennett with his quirky distinctive walk and his twirling cane. His character had a put upon, everyman quality much like Buster Keaton. But Charlie's tramp had a certain tinge of roguishness that Keaton's sweet tempered persona did not. A tramp might be expected to steal or be a law breaker. He was at heart an anarchist and that was the essence of the character. From then on the role was called the Little Tramp. Chaplin played his alter ego in a side splitting series of silent films that, true to his boast, made him a familiar name to everyone in America.

Charlie had preferred sitting in the comfortable salon car to the solitude of his sleeping compartment. He enjoyed meeting and talking to other passengers. He was not the only celebrity on the train for Detroit. The Secretary of Commerce, Herbert Hoover, member of President Coolidge's cabinet was also on board. Charlie encountered him the first evening dining in the club car. They had not met before but instantly recognized one another. It was not long before they shared a conversation about current events. Although Charlie was an Englishman, he had a broad knowledge of American politics. He had been active selling War bonds and had made numerous public appearances on behalf of the war effort. Hoover was a Republican, a prominent engineer and business man who in five years would be elected the 31st President of the United States. He possessed a keen analytical mind and a technical knowledge that impressed Charlie even if he found his subject somewhat dry. Hoover was convinced as his boss, President Coolidge was, that it was big business that was responsible for American prosperity. He believed the best that government could do was enact legislation favorable to business interests, then get out of the way. Charlie, who in later years would be accused of Communist sympathies, disagreed heartily with much of what Hoover held. Many of those themes would surface in his later movies: *City Lights* and *Modern Times*. Charlie, like many artists, took a dim view of capitalism. He felt it was inherently inhumane. It reduced humans to mere implements of progress rather than beneficiaries. Hoover, for his part, believed capitalism was the great organizing principle of American society. He argued that if all individuals were free to pursue their own self-interest unimpeded by government, humanity achieved its full potential as if directed by the force of an invisible hand. This exposed the fundamental difference between their schools of thought. Despite their differences, they shared an interesting and cordial conversation. They also discovered they would both be staying at the Statler Hotel in Detroit.

The afternoon of their arrival at Michigan Central Station, Charlie noticed a large crowd milling about the platform. Several porters approached asking to assist him with his luggage. The scene when he left the train and headed into the terminal was of great excitement. A large crowd had turned out to welcome him and were laughing and applauding. He beamed at the crowd and waved expansively. He shook a few hands as he acknowledged their ovation.

Hoover exited the train a few moments after Charlie. The platform was empty and he searched with vexation for someone to fetch his luggage. He walked into the terminal just in time to see the crowd of well-wishers surrounding Chaplin. He was not an overly vain man but the embarrassment he felt at that moment would be noticed and reported by the Detroit Free Press the next day. Hoover would have his vindication 5 years later when he collected Michigan's 15 electoral votes on the way to winning the Presidency. But this day clearly belonged to Charlie Chaplin.

Chaplin clearly enjoyed his whirlwind tour. He was feted at a luncheon at the Statler Hotel where he lifted his glass and roguishly toasted his audience: "Well boys, here's to crime" which brought a roar of laughter. He went on to expound about the importance of art and the power of laughter to elevate the human condition. He reminisced about this earlier visit to Detroit years before. After lunch he was conducted on visits to a number of local high schools. At each stop he was greeted with excitement and acclaim by the students and their teachers.

The highlight of this visit was to the Highland Park assembly plant for a personal tour conducted by Henry and Edsel Ford. The Free Press reported that the elder Ford remarked he had come from his office in Dearborn to see him, a distance of ten miles. Charlie remarked, good naturedly, he had come halfway across the country to meet Ford. The paper reported the tour was very cordial and Charlie observed with great interest the impressive machinery that powered the assembly line. He was astonished how the vehicles rolled off the end of the line with such fast paced regularity. Almost like sausages, Charlie thought to himself.

The observations that Charlie made that day would be recreated years later in his classic film, *Modern Times*. Chaplin's beloved little Tramp would be placed in an industrial setting with hilarious results. Chaplin with his keen sensibilities and light hearted touch made the grinding pace and dehumanizing monotony of the factory serve as background, not the focus, of his comic misadventures. It gave an affectionate view of how an audacious and resourceful person could survive the demands of modern times. The symbolism was secondary to the humor. That was Chaplin's genius.

Chaplin's career had a long way to go when left Detroit on an east bound train for the next stop on his cross country tour. He would successfully transition from silent to talking picture. But along the way he would run afoul of another Hoover (J. Edgar). He would be placed under a cloud of suspicion as an undesirable alien with communist sympathies, and a notorious libertine with an unhealthy affection for much younger women.

The accusations and suspicion that dogged his later career would serve as a background for his considerable artistic achievements. In a clear case of life imitating art, the struggles against legal problems, bad publicity, and waning popularity provided context for his comic creations. Just as in his classic film *Modern Times* the viewer felt, when pitted against the unrelenting gears of brutish circumstance, Charley Chaplin would find a way to turn the outcome inevitably towards laughter.

Whistle Stop 15

NOVEMBER 23, 1941

The Countess

The woman would attract attention even when attempting to appear inconspicuous. In her 30s, slim, attractive, dressed in fashionable, expensive clothing, glittering with jewelry; she would turn the head of any middle aged male who happened to spot her. Tonight she was unconcerned about any attention she might receive. She had learned well the skills of hiding in plain sight and was adept at them. Indeed her whole image was fashioned on being seen and recognized in the fashionable, influential circles in which she ran. She met the best people there, the most knowledgeable people, the most useful people. And it was this very usefulness that she was cultivating for her employers. Her name was Grace-Buchanan Dineen known to her friends and admirers as the Countess. Tonight she was in route to her new home in Detroit where she had been sent by her superiors on a mission of great importance. The Countess was an agent of Nazi intelligence assigned to Detroit to spy on the "Arsenal of Democracy".

The train carrying her from New York arrived in Michigan Central at 11:15 PM. She had been booked on a flight out of New York the next morning. At the last minute she bought a train ticket to arrive a day earlier. She phoned ahead to the hotel changing her reservation for her earlier arrival and arranging for a driver to pick her up at the train station. She was absolutely certain that no one knew she was coming at that time or place. She felt perfectly secure she would arrive in Detroit unobserved. The unexpected arrival would also give her a change to execute the next part of her plan. The traffic in the railroad terminal at this time of night should be very light. The Japanese attack on Pearl Harbor was still weeks away and as yet the peace sentiment in the nation remained strong so there was little apprehension about enhanced security. German intelligence was not content to wait for the outbreak of hostilities and was already actively assembling a network of spies to keep an eye on developments in America. No one could predict when the tension would erupt into warfare but the Nazis would be ready.

There was virtually no one there in the station when she collected her luggage. A solitary porter helped her load the leather bags onto a cart. Joshua Holloway, the porter, was loitering in the station waiting for his own departure for Buffalo later that evening. With nothing better to do and a little time to kill, he cheerfully offered to conduct her baggage to her waiting vehicle outside the station. She gratefully accepted his offer. The absence of people was good; that was what she expected. She would not meet her assigned contact for two days. In the meantime she would be staying at the Statler Hotel. It was well known for its luxurious accommodations and celebrity clientele. It suited her tastes.

Before leaving the station, she made a stop at the long term storage lockers; used to store parcels or small objects, as a convenience for travelers. Josh politely waited outside the office. The solitary clerk working the over-night shift seemed surprised to have a customer at this late hour; usually he kept busy filing and cleaning. But he took the sealed parcel she produced and placed it into a safety deposit box. The attendant issued a claim check and a key. She paid the storage fee in advance for a year and placed her key and claim check into her purse. She was being cautious to go to such lengths to store this information; but it eliminated the risk of being found with incriminating evidence in her possession. She also anticipated a poten-tial need for a quick getaway so it was useful to store her information close to an outbound train. Most importantly it gave her a measure of leverage and protection from the two opposing groups who would be most inter-ested in possessing this material- the FBI and German Intelligence. The information in the lock box, given to the FBI, was a valuable bargaining chip which might buy leniency for her. The Nazis would stop at nothing to keep this information safely out of hands of the Feds. She knew the risk if ever she became a loose end they needed to tie up. She understood intuitively, what a dangerous game she was playing. This secret trove of evidence would be an effective insurance policy that just might keep her alive. The evidence in storage was already preaddressed and postage paid for delivery to the *Detroit Free Press*. If she was ever on the run, she could take the envelope from the safety deposit box and drop it in the mail slot at the terminal. If everything worked out, she would simply leave this ma-terial safely hidden. If she needed to move it to another hiding place she could do so whenever she wanted. As long as she paid the box rental fee, her material was safe. For now she felt sure she had covered all her tracks. She led Josh to the waiting limousine from the Statler outside the terminal.

The story of how Grace became a German spy went back years ago to her youth in Toronto. She was the heiress to a fur and clothier business established by her grandfather. When the business failed and her parents divorced, young Grace was taken by her father to live in Europe. Grace enjoyed the gracious lifestyle of the well-heeled café society. It was here she first used the "Countess" pose. She traced her nobility back to an alleged French count from the last century. Her posed patrician pedigree, great beauty, and stunning wardrobe were all she needed. She had very shortly made acquaintances with very influential people from all over the continent. In Budapest she met a woman of her own age and similar background, a Hungarian national and graduate of Vassar named Sari De Hajek. She and her husband had lived in the states and spied for the German government before being deported. It was this couple who recruited Grace, and in exchange for an advance of $2500 and a promise of $500 a month, Grace began her career in espionage. She was schooled in all the dark skills of spy craft in Germany. She learned how to make and use invisible ink, the basics of micro-photography, and how to develop and maintain a convincing cover that would screen her true occupation. She also was taught how the information she collected was to be forwarded to Germany.

Her assignment had been two fold. First she was to gather as much intelligence as she could on the Ford Motor Company's potential war production. This also included assessing the company's vulnerability to sabotage. Detroit's enormous industrial capacity was an object of great concern for the Nazis. Plants were already producing trucks for delivery to America's European allies. Soon vast numbers of tanks and airplanes would be rolling off the assembly lines of the Motor City. There was a wealth of information to be gained by the Germans by having eyes and ears on this massive complex. In addition, the vast flow of shipping through the Great Lakes was of interest to the Third Reich. If these shipping routes could be closed, the assembly plants dependent on the free flow of commodities would be crippled. Several intelligence agencies in Berlin were focused exclusively on this vital component of the Allied war machine.

The second part of her mission was to make contact with agents already in place to coordinate their efforts and increase the amount of intelligence going to Berlin. The names and addresses of nearly 200 individuals scattered through the Midwest known to be German sympathizers or active agents were written in a small black and green checked notebook which now resided in a safety deposit box in Michigan Central Station.

Grace's contact in Detroit was Teresa Behrens She and her husbands were naturalized citizens of Yugoslavian descent, and devout Nazis. She worked as a secretary for the International YWCA which placed her in frequent contact with immigrants. She used her influence to disseminate Nazi ideology whenever she could. She on occasion would recruit likely candidates for her work. She had in turn introduced Grace to Dr. Fred W. Thomas, surgeon and obstetrician, who was an active member of the German Bund, a large group of American citizens of German descent and Nazi sympathies. Another pair of established spies was Marianna Von Moltke, a real life countess of German descent and her husband, a suspended Wayne State University professor. The inner circle of Grace's spy ring was rounded out by Emma and Carl Leonhardt who operated a rooming house on Garland Avenue that became the rings safe house and meeting place. Factories all over the Midwest became targets of their espionage. Grace, from her apartment on East Jefferson would regularly collect and forward the information to German intelligence. She would employ normal correspondence but use invisible ink to write coded information on the page. The dispatch was then forwarded to one of several mail drops in neutral countries, often Portugal, where it would be retrieved by German couriers. This process turned out to be Grace's undoing.

All Pan Am Clippers to and from Europe were required to land in Bermuda. There any transatlantic correspondence had to be inspected by British counter intelligence agents. Over time, a number of addresses in Europe began to arouse suspicion as being a front for German intelligence traffic. One of these addresses had been used by Grace. The British then used special chemical agents to reveal any invisible ink writing concealed on the page. Once an espionage document was identified, the long careful process began to trace the document back to its writer. Since there was no return address on the letter, the only clue was the postmark from Detroit.

In addition to that, the stationary and envelope were carefully analyzed for any clues to the origin of the letter. Using these tools, an anonymous person in Detroit code named: "Miss Smith" was soon identified. Next came the gum shoe work of finding her. The process of unmasking Grace would take months of effort as FBI agents descended on Detroit to pursue every lead.

Grace had hidden the claim check and key to her safety deposit box in a place she was certain it would never be found. A devout and practicing Catholic, she had noticed in St Anne's Church one Sunday morning, a statue of the Virgin Mary residing in a secluded alcove of the church separating two confessionals. At the back of the icon, she found a narrow space between the statues base and the carved wooden stand on which is rested. She was just able to insert the small envelope containing the key and claim check into that space. Using a nail file, she pushed it back far enough that it could not be seen. She genuflected in front of the Madonna, crossed herself and withdrew.

By the time the FBI had tracked her down; Grace's ring had been operating for over a year. But finally the FBI's diligence paid off and Grace-Buchanan Dineen was identified as the mysterious "Miss Smith". The FBI had her under close observation but did not immediately arrest her. They hoped she would lead them to her confederates. It was on Sunday morning after mass, Grace was observed kneeling in devotion in front of a statue of the Madonna when the agents noticed some strange behavior. Grace after carefully looking around to see if she was being watched, circled the statue and carefully began probing at its base with what appeared to be a small blade. This errand was completed quickly. She genuflected in front of the Madonna, crossed herself and left without a backward glance.

The FBI agents immediately began inspecting the statue and in very short order had discovered Grace's hiding place. The parcel was removed from its safety deposit box in Michigan Central within the hour, and by that evening Grace-Buchanan Dineen was arrested and charged with espionage. "Third degree" (a euphuism for torture) methods of interrogation were not used on Grace. When confronted with the evidence, she was isolated in a small room with no windows and a pack of cigarettes to think things over. The FBI had given her one chance. If she would agree to begin working for them she would be given preferential treatment and a lighter sentence at her eventual trial. Since her one bargaining chip was taken away, Grace had no choice but to become a double agent. The FBI used her to transmit information they wanted the Germans to receive, all of it carefully designed to mislead them. The spy ring she headed continued to function and actually met dozens of times after Grace had been compromised and flipped. All the individuals in Grace's notebook were now being carefully watched. Grace went about her life, still under the cover of a fashionable Detroit socialite. She met and fell in love with a prominent Detroit businessman, Nelson E. Butler, and they were engaged to be married. Grace kept her true identity from her fiancée.

On August 24 1943, the FBI was ready to move. All the inner circle of Grace's spy ring was arrested. At trial, her testimony was instrumental in the government's case against her co-defendants. Sentences for the convicted ranged from five to twenty years. Grace as the ringleader, was sentence to twelve years. This was considered severe since she had been helpful in making the government's case. Grace was sent to a women's correctional facility in West Virginia to serve her sentence. Her devoted fiancée, who vowed to wait for her, had visited frequently during her in-carceration. Sadly, while she was still imprisoned, she learned of his death from a heart attack. Grace was heartbroken. Within a month of his death, Grace's sentence was commuted by President Truman to nine years which made her eligible for early parole. Her release required immediate deporta-tion to Canada. It was on a train to Toronto that Grace-Buchanan Dineen was lost to history. The date of her death remains unknown,

Whistle Stop 16

NOVEMBER 2, 1941

The Unions

The hostility between the Brotherhood of Railway Clerks and the powerful Teamsters Union had been heating up for some time. The dispute was primarily a turf war involving boundaries between the two labor unions. Many of the types of jobs represented by the Brotherhood also fell under the Teamsters banner. Both of the rival organizations competed against each other for members among a single body of workers. The simmering conflict had been provoked by a recent National Mediation Board (NMB) ruling in favor of the Railway Clerk's right to collective bargaining. The NMB ruling overturned a District

Court opposing the Clerks. The victory of the Brotherhood was viewed as a primal threat to the dominance of the Teamsters, who angrily voiced their opposition and planned retribution. The Railway Clerks had recently ended their month long strike to return to work, only to be met with a strong Teamsters picket line. A minor scuffle ensued in which one worker was injured. But the stage was set for a more violent conflict which erupted the next morning.

Early on Saturday morning, members the Brotherhood attempted to move several trucks from Michigan Central's loading docks. The Teamsters insisted in the investigation conducted in the aftermath that these trucks were not molested in any way by the Teamster picketers. They testified the departing trucks instead of leaving the scene drove to the end of the street and stopped, blocking the Teamsters escape. A swarm of the Clerks, armed with baseball bats attacked the Teamsters from both the loading docks and the trucks. In the ensuing melee in which the Clerks greatly outnumbered their rivals, five cars were smashed to pieces. An unmarked police car arrived on the scene and was also attacked and destroyed. After a pitched battle, ten police cars and patrol wagons arrived on the scene to restore order, and forced the Clerks to retreat. Even after they withdrew to the loading docks they still brandished their baseball bats waiting for another outbreak of fighting. It was very clear the violence would not end with this single outbreak.

The carnage inflicted on that day sent at least eight of the rioters to the hospital with skull fractures and closed head injuries, several of them critical. At least 5 were arrested and charged with assault. Several of the Brotherhood leadership were charged with inciting a riot and malicious destruction of properly. This would be merely the opening rounds of a running dispute between the two unions. There had been union violence before in Detroit and there would be again. Most of the time the disputes were between management and labor and involved higher pay or better working conditions. In this case the violence was unusual as it was between two labor unions each protecting its own interests from the other. Detroit's history of labor relations has often been acrimonious with thuggery and intimidation part of the negotiation process. In time labor was increasingly viewed as a legitimate partner in industry and its leadership grew more professional. Confrontation among rivals would mostly be resolved in the courts rather than the workplace. But on this particular day a vicious brawl was the unfortunate mediator.

Whistle Stop 17

MAY 18, 1967

The 1967 Riot (Part 1) Jackson

The end of the war in 1945 returned boom times to Detroit. After the delayed gratification of the war, the Arsenal of Democracy was transformed quickly to make way for peacetime production. The economy quickly surged to satisfy the pent up demand for housing, automobiles, and consumer goods. Predictably, the auto industry led the way with the iconic Big Three domestic manufacturers dominating the global industry. As these titans prospered, Detroit enjoyed the benefits. Jobs were plentiful with hordes of returning service men trading in the tools of the trade of warfare for employment on the assembly lines of the

Motor City. The new workforce set about mass producing automobiles and babies at astonishing rates. The cars they built found new roads to drive on when the Eisenhower administration launched a massive highway construction project which created the interstate highway system. Originally proposed as a vital defense initiative, the innovative roads were soon flooded with recreational and commercial traffic. American's passion for travel was stimulated by higher wages and more leisure. "Going like 60" became a familiar idiom to describe people racing headlong into the future, most frequently in their own cars. Paradoxically, as more people were on the move, the traffic on the nation's railways was stagnating. Increasingly, consumers found traveling by car or airplane cheaper, faster, and more attractive than riding the rails, as had been done for the first half of the twentieth century. Not yet finished, but the future of travel in the United States was moving away from railroads. Michigan Central Station was beginning to experience the technological obsolescence of an industry whose time was passing. There would be many such extinction events spanning the entire breath of the economy in the decades following the war. Restless innovators constantly reinvent commerce. In the end, the strongest and most adaptable enterprises survive by natural selection, and the rest recede into history.

Equally consequential as the economic recovery were the changes in global politics that were transforming American society in fundamental ways. The early post-war years were marked by residual conflict between the former allies giving way to the political and military tension of the Cold War and the nuclear arms race. The massive accomplishments of the Berlin Airlift, the Marshall Plan and the NATO alliance succeeded in stabilizing Europe in an uneasy equilibrium thwarting Soviet expansionism. On the other side of the planet the regional aspirations of the Chinese communists erupted in Korea and Vietnam with continuing warfare for many more bloody years. Inexorably, through these tumultuous years, the United States role of undisputed leader of the free world accelerated. Not lost on the black community was the irony that so many American citizens were systematically and legally denied the same freedoms championed by their government elsewhere in the world.

At the same time, the post-war world seemed to embrace a renewed sense of mutualism where prosperity and security were pursued in a cooperative manner among nations. This went far beyond the military alliances that had congealed European politics during much of the 20th century. The founding of the United Nations with its offspring World Bank and World Health Organization, International Monetary Fund and General Agreement on Tariffs and Trade (GATT) were recognition that to secure lasting peace, the nations must work together on common problems. Equally important, a commission on Human Rights was established trying to elevate the attention paid to that critical issue, especially in nations for which human rights had never been a priority. As well intentioned as these initiatives were, they did little to improve the daily lives of millions of black families like the Holloways living in the United States.

The Truman years were devoted to honoring commitments made during the war. One of the most pressing was to reward military veterans for their service. The passage of the GI bill provided broad assistance but southern Democrats in Congress made certain the benefits of education and housing would not reach the black community. When Eisenhower became president, the tidal wave of the Baby Boom was cresting creating explosive growth in the standard of living. The rising tide of prosperity, contrary to the old saying did not raise all boats. The vessels of the black community seemed to have less buoyancy. Since emancipation, black citizens had never fully participated in the benefits of a growing economy, while Jim Crow laws and segregation persisted in the South. Even the historic Supreme Court decision in 1954, Brown vs the Board of Education, which struck down the "Separate but Equal" clause that justified school segregation, did not fully rectify the inequality. At the dawn of the 1960's the administration of the young and idealistic John Kennedy began belatedly to turn inwards proposing fundamental changes to the law to eradicate the last remnants of racism. The promise of racial harmony did not excite the voters nearly as much as the commitment to a Moon Landing within the decade. An assassin's bullet in Dallas put an end to the hopes for civil rights legislation in 1963. It would be up to Lyndon Johnson, a southerner, to finally preside over the passage of the Civil Rights Act of 1964 and The Voting Rights Act of 1965. Johnson called his sweeping initiatives the "Great Society". Like the New Deal before, it promised transformative action to fundamentally change the role of government. Central to these changes was a so called War on Poverty which increased spending in education, health care, housing, and transportation, much of which was targeted at the black community. Johnson famously quoted the civil rights anthem, when in a speech; he proclaimed, "We shall overcome". What the New Deal had done to ensure economic security, the Great Society aspired to do for social justice and civil rights. Not everyone welcomed these changes, of course; spawning decades of discord. Overnight American regional political allegiances were upended. The "Solid South" of dependable Democratic States became the political base of the Republican Party. Twenty of the next 24 years would see the GOP occupy the White House. Ultimately, Johnson would be revered by history for his domestic achievements even while enduring intense criticism for the foreign policy quagmire in Vietnam which prematurely ended his presidency in 1968.

The Brown decision had inspired the Civil Rights Movement and new leaders in the black community emerged. In 1955, Rosa Parks launched the Montgomery Bus boycott simply by her refusal to give up her seat to white passengers. This important event in turn elevated to prominence an eloquent Baptist preacher from Atlanta, Dr. Martin Luther King Jr. whose voice would sear the conscience of a nation. King embraced a nonviolent activism inspired by Mahatma Gandhi, the father of the Indian nation who agitated for change against British colonial rule, but never resorted to bloodshed. King's work in turn motivated a host of other dedicated civil rights workers who agreed with his approach-among them Ralph Abernathy, John Lewis, Jesse Jackson, Andrew Young, Bernard Lee and hosts of others. Some militant Black leaders, among them the contro-versial Malcom X, decried the slow pace of change and denounced this "gradualism" in favor of a more confrontational movement. His powerful pronouncement that Black Nationalism must be pursued "by any means necessary" put him at odds with King. Ironically, despite their differences, both leaders were destined to meet similar violent ends. Malcom was assassinated in New York City in 1965, a victim of disaffected Nation of Islam members who had turned against him, wielding a sawed off shotgun and semi-automatic pistols. In 1968 in Memphis, Dr. King added his name to the list of martyrs for civil rights, stuck down by an assassin's bullet. His murderer, a small time hoodlum and avowed racist, James Earl Ray, would be sentenced to ninety nine years for the crime and would survive in prison until 1998. Being an advocate was dangerous work, but the horrors of assassination, church bombings and lynching were not reserved for politically prominent black Americans. Over four thousand seven hundred lynchings occurred in the USA from 1882 to 1968. A disproportionately high number of these were poor black citizens whose names are mostly unremembered in history. This sad record remains a stain on the nation's legacy and reputation that will never be bleached clean. Despite coming from very different ideological viewpoints, both Malcom and Dr. King were well aware how far short our nation had fallen to live up to the ideal that "all men are created equal". Both, despite the disparity of their methods, sought the long denied freedom and equality for their community. Both etched their names indelibly upon the turbulent history of the times.

Within this period of great historical ferment, the Holloway cousins, Jackson and Julius, came of age in Detroit. In many ways their lives were very different than their fathers but in some ways were fundamentally unchanged. Both lived in segregated communities as had their fathers and were well acquainted with racial prejudice. But both boys were raised in more prosperous circumstances than their fathers. Josh and Clem Holloway, began their lives as sharecroppers in Mississippi in the Jim Crow south. Both had come to Detroit before the war in search of a better life. Josh had found success in the growing Detroit music industry as a performer and impresario while Clem, an auto worker, had fallen victim to the violence of the riots of 1943. Jackson's mother Althea had remarried eight years after Clem's death to a good man,

Tom Simmons, owner and operator of *The Rooster*, a restaurant in Paradise Valley just off Hastings. That neighborhood was slowly being fragmented by freeway construction and urban development. The already poor area seemed to be sinking even deeper into the blight of the inner city. Still, with Althea as the chef, she and her new husband were able to prosper at the Rooster serving the remaining community a menu of Soul and Cajun dishes Althea had learned growing up in Louisiana. Althea's former father in law George, Clem's father, and Jackson's grandfather, long retired from the auto industry was on hand to help run the business. He handled the maintenance on the property and equipment and supervised the daily cleaning routine. He also did the daily shopping for the seafood, meat, and produce hauling it in his old pick up every morning from the Eastern Market off Gratiot Avenue. Jackson grew up serving as everything from busboy, to waiter, to dishwasher.

Jackson had been a diffident student in elementary school. Althea worked with him constantly to improve his academic skills and self-confidence. As he grew he became increasingly aware of the tragic circumstances of his father's death. Though he had never known his Dad, he became highly motivated by his desire to live up to his memory. By the time he arrived at Cass Tech High School, he had blossomed into a promising scholar and athlete. Students were required to maintain good grades for eligibility to play sports, and Jackson was mad for sports, especially football. He was blessed with blazing speed and was highly sought after by the school's football coach, for the backfield of the Technicians squad. After a spectacular four years of athletic success and solid academic performance he was ready to attend college. There was never a doubt in his mind where he wished to matriculate. As a young boy he had watched an Independence Day parade in Detroit. He had been enthralled by the sight of black servicemen resplendent in uniform passing in procession bearing the colors, the sunlight gleaming off their meticulously polished brass buttons and buckles. He had resolved then and there to join their ranks as soon as he was able. Jackson Holloway would become a soldier. The United States Military Academy at West Point was his dream destination.

With the help and support of his family and coaches and teachers from Cass Tech, Jackson secured an appointment from his congressman, a long-standing friend of the family who had been a former pastor of their family since the war. There was great excitement among the entire Holloway clan as the day for his departure for West Point approached. Like many momentous passages of the Holloway clan this life changing journey would begin at Michigan Central Station. Despite the longer transit time, the railways were symbolically at least, the mode of transport preferred by the family. This dedication to train travel always recalled how his uncle Josh had escaped the oppression of the South in his younger days. A tremendous sendoff party at the Rooster was attended by scores of well-wishers. George, his grandfather, and great uncle Cyrus all the way from Mississippi, both gave emotional speeches calling to mind Jackson's father Clem and how proud he would have been to see this day. Jackson had been overwhelmed by the tearful outpouring of love and support. Toward the end of the evening, as the guests were beginning to leave, he was irresistibly drawn to his cousin Julius, The two, born only months apart had been raised more as twin brothers than cousins. Next to leaving his mother, this was the most painful parting of all. The two had shared their deepest hopes and fears for their entire lives and both thought of each other as hero and role model. Now the current of their lives was sweeping them in different directions but they pledged, whatever the circumstances, to be there for each other through the years. Both understood their lives were inextricably bound together. This mutual dependency would become important in years to come.

1961 Beast Barracks United States Military Academy

The United Stated Military Academy, like much of the nation, had an ambiguous history of race relations. The first black cadet to graduate and be commissioned as an officer was Henry Ossian Flipper, a former slave who was appointed to West Point during the tumultuous days of Southern Reconstruction. Flipper joined four other black cadets who were already in attendance. All faced rejection from their classmates and had a difficult time adjusting to the suffocating regimentation. Flipper was the first of this group to graduate in 1877. After leaving West Point he was assigned to the 10th Calvary Regiment at Fort Concho in west Texas. He became the first non-white officer to command an all-Black Buffalo Soldier Regiment. He saw distinguished service in action during the Apache Wars running the notorious war chief, Victorio, to ground. Despite his record for competence in command, his career was marred by several episodes. One involved a friendship with the sister in law of his company commander, a white man named Captain Nicholas Nolan. Nolan defended his subordinate against any suspicion of impropriety by describing him to be as much "an officer and a gentleman" as any white man in his command. Still the rest of his fellow officers remained suspicious and hostile. Flipper ultimately ran afoul of another commander, William Shafter who accused him of embezzling over 2,000 dollars from the quartermaster's safe. Many suspected the entire affair to be a set up that was racially motivated. So highly esteemed was Flipper that the soldiers in his unit and members of the community donated funds to cover the shortage in just four days. Shafter accepted the donations but had Flipper court martialed anyway. He was acquitted on the charges of theft but convicted of a vague "conduct unbecoming" charge and dishonorably discharged. This stain on his record would remain until 1999 when his case would be reviewed and his dishonorable discharge was overturned. Shortly thereafter a plaque was erected on the campus at West Point and an award instituted in Flippers name, The Henry O. Flipper award is given annually to the graduating cadet best exemplifying "leadership, self-discipline, and perseverance in the face of unusual difficulties." West Point has come to terms with it's past at least belatedly.

Jackson Holloway's plebe class included six other black cadets. Assignments within the class were divided into separate regiments and interaction with different regiments was very limited so there was not much chance to interact with his fellows. The physical rigors of Beast Barracks where the first-years endured a hellish basic training were not a problem for the superbly conditioned athletic Jackson. The academics were more challenging and his first exposure to calculus was demoralizing. If it had not been for the growing friendship with a white bunkmate, Roy Baxter, who was a wiz at math, Jackson would never have made it. Jackson learned several years later Baxter's parents had been asked specifically beforehand, whether they had any objection to their son rooming with a black student but had consented. This discovery both annoyed and saddened Jackson but he did not blame Roy or his parents. He was deeply disappointed in West Point officials.

The demands of the classroom did at least fill the time that he would otherwise have devoted to sports. In all the years of Academy football, there had never been a black player on the varsity team. It would be another five years before that barrier would be broken by Gary Steele a tight end with 220 pounds of muscle stretched over his 6'5" frame and blessed with great speed and soft hands. Sadly, that landmark would come too late for Jackson Holloway. But he was so busy with his studies he almost stopped missing football. He enjoyed cheering for the Black Knights on autumn afternoons in Michie Stadium. Frustratingly, his stay at the Academy was during the glory years of Navy football. Joe Bellino and Roger Staubach, both Heisman trophy winners, were the stars of those teams in the 1960s. Much to the dismay of the Army faithful, the Knights suffered ignominious defeats repeatedly during that decade. Deep down he felt deprived of one of his true passions and he earnestly believed he could have made a difference in the outcome of some of those losses. The pain of that lost opportunity would subside but never disappear.

By the time Jackson arrived, West Point was relatively free of overt racism. Even though the number of Black cadets was always small in proportion to total enrollment, the stress and demands placed on all cadets were so encompassing that few had time or energy for bigotry. There was a feeling of esprit that joined the students in common cause against the great demands imposed by the school. This was precisely the kind of mutual trust that the Army would need to build into its officer corps to fight futures wars. Jackson made a number of devoted friends with whom he would remain close for the rest of his life. The bonds of respect and friendship and the leadership skills forged during his Academy days would be put to the test in a matter of months. Jackson graduated near the middle of his class in 1964 and received his commission as a second lieutenant in the United States Army. Like many of his classmates he was bound for service in Vietnam.

Saigon Vietnam September 1966

Jackson's first impression of Vietnam was sweltering heat and humidity, and streets swarming with pedestrians, massive numbers of scooters, bicycles, and motorcycles. Jackson noticed a farmer patiently prodding a huge bovine through the bedlam, hitched to a cart piled high with melons and pineapple. Everyone seemed to be in a hurry to reach their destinations. Countless military convoys clogged the roadways along with a few private civilian automobiles. American GIs as well as ARVN troops (South Vietnamese Army) were seen virtually everywhere providing a sense of security for a city where the enemy could not so easily be recognized and was capable of disappearing quickly into the vast crowds. The atmosphere buzzed with the chaotic jumble familiar to any big city during rush hour. Despite the violent conflict underlying all this commotion there was an undeniable sense of commerce and prosperity. Indeed, the presence of the United States military brought a most welcome influx of money into the economy and the hotels, bars, restaurants, and brothels reaped the rewards of thriving business. The posh Rex Hotel downtown was the unofficial headquarters where military brass, the press, and diplomatic officials all congregated while overseeing the daily business of war, frequently from the scenic roof top bar overlooking the city's busiest intersection. Despite the violence and uncertain political environment, Saigon was clearly focused on the work of earning a living. The existential threat of warfare was a barely suppressed distraction that the local population did their best to ignore. The plight of working people is usually more dependent on resourcefulness and personal industry than on those who happen to be in charge. Whoever controlled the government, the people were determined to avoid trouble and to go on living. Detroit was the biggest city Jackson had seen before but it seemed compact and orderly compared to Saigon.

Jackson, like many of his fellows was fairly nonpolitical. He had made an effort to familiarize himself with Vietnamese history and culture, even took an introductory course in the language before he left school. Still he was politically unsophisticated and not adequately prepared for life on the ground or the daily, dangerous routine of a soldier. He would learn these things soon enough. For the moment, his belief system was formed on the bedrock of faith in his country. If his orders said he should fight dangerous enemies in this remote place that was enough for him.

Jackson was assigned to the 1st Cavalry Division as a platoon leader. In early days the Cavalry were horse mounted soldiers whose greater mobility compared to the infantry made them invaluable for quick deployment and recon. In Vietnam this mobility was provided by a huge fleet of helicopters. Many of these airships were the workhorse HU-1 nicknamed Hueys. They provided the capabilities of horse mounted troops on the ground while also serving as a platform for an array of lethal armament. This weaponry complimented the attack helicopter's other uses as a troop carrier, medivac, search and rescue, and reconnaissance craft. Jackson had grown up watching Western movies where the arrival of rescuing soldiers was signaled by pounding hooves. In Vietnam that welcome sound was replaced by the whoosh of chopper blades. Either way, to beleaguered troops on the ground, it sounded like help was on the way.

Jackson soon settled into the daily routine. His platoon consisted of mostly draftees from all over the US. More than half of the soldiers in his company were black teenagers but there seemed to be little racial tension in the ranks. Jackson had heard that was not always the case and counted himself lucky he would not have to deal with that. Despite being a combat unit much of their time was spent waiting for orders to move out. Their assigned barracks was hot and crowded and the food was bland. Too much time on their hands contributed to lax discipline. Soldiers with little else to do, found ready diversion in recreational marijuana and hashish which always seemed to be in supply. There was also enough beer available to quench the thirst of idle soldiers in the field. Jackson was vigilant in discouraging and punishing troops for drug and alcohol abuse. But it was so widespread that it could not be stopped entirely. The Army understood draftees were often disorderly compared to professional soldiers. Still they did their best to maintain discipline and combat readiness. In this platoon that responsibility fell on 2nd Lieutenant Jackson Holloway. Jackson, displaying the leadership skills polished at the academy, performed his duties well and was respected by his men. When the call came, his troops would be ready.

In short order, the platoon was assigned patrol duties in the nearby bush surrounding their base. Even though these missions never required patrolling great distances or bivouacking in the field, or risked encountering large enemy deployments, they were nevertheless fraught with danger from booby-traps and land mines placed by their invisible enemies. It was nerve racking duty walking these perilous trails through the dense tropical growth, achingly alert for any sudden sound or movement. Jackson's platoon suffered a number of injuries from these patrols, but thankfully no one was killed.

One of the soldiers in his platoon frequently drew Jackson's attention. Arturo Molina was not a disobedient soldier but he bore an air of menace that isolated him from the rest of his unit. He towered over all of his mates in the company standing 6'6" and was powerfully built. He was known among the other boots in his outfit simply as "Big A". He had a sullen personality and did not seem to have any friends in the unit. No one doubted his nerve or brains but he just seemed too tightly wound and apt to explode at any time, the kind of dangerous man well suited for dangerous work. Jackson learned that Big A, like himself, was a Detroit native and that gave him something to relate to with the introverted soldier. He never got too much additional information from Molina. Jackson never really warmed to his subordinate but for reasons he could not explain resolved to keep the big man nearby when they inevitably would be called into combat.

Their turn came in early 1966 when a massive search and destroy mission was ordered in Binh Dinh Province on the central coastal plain of South Vietnam. This area was known to be infiltrated by Viet Cong and a dangerous threat to the whole region. The high command made the tactical decision to clear them out. This mission was code named Operation Masher and would be a coordinated attack by units of the ARVN and ROK (Republic of Korea) under the leadership of the American 1st Cavalry Division. Jackson Holloway was about to have his fiery baptism leading men in battle.

The operation was very simple. The American forces aided by their allies would encircle the concentrations of enemy troops and Viet Cong guerillas and destroy them. In a battle for the hearts and minds of a population it was always hard to have an objective measurement of success regardless of how many battles you won. In Vietnam the sole objective measurement was the body count, the brutal daily scorekeeping of enemy dead. In the perverse logic of warfare, when the enemy was all killed, the hearts and minds of those left alive would follow.

The ensuing firefight that engulfed Jackson's platoon took place in a row of ridges cleft by a deep ravine. A force of Viet Cong fighters opened fire with small arms, machine guns, and mortars an hour after the Americans had arrived on the scene in their squadron of Hueys. Not anticipating heavy resistance, the helicopters had offloaded and returned to base. The heavy fighting that had erupted throughout the entire sector resulted in air support being spread thin, meaning that Jackson's platoon could not expect any immediate help from the air. For the moment, his command was on its own. For two horrible hours the battle on the ground raged all around them. Jackson had heard the expression "the fog of battle" but never completely understood until now the blind confusion and sheer paralysis of judgement suffered by men in combat. In those awful moments the most powerful impulse was to turn and run for your lives. Jackson's training and leadership at the decisive moment took hold and he was able to rally his troops to hold their position. He deployed them behind the cover of a shallow ditch lined with low thick bush. From that position they could see the enemy movements across an open field 50 meters away. One of his men had been hit and lay exposed in the field separating the two lines of fire. Seized by an impulse that for years later he could never explain, Jackson broke from cover and raced, dodging enemy strafing as he ran, to rescue the fallen soldier. He was hit in the thigh just above his knee as he closed the distance and fell into the scant protection of a shallow shell crater. The pain exploded like a bomb in his brain before he blacked out. At that moment, Arturo Molina broke into the clearing like a crazed man, screaming like a banshee, firing his M-16 in short bursts as he raced towards Jackson's position. He paused long enough to hurl a grenade towards the enemy line, an impossibly long distance away. The bomb traveled nearly 30 meters in the air and landed on top of a machine gun nest. He hunched over, hit in the shoulder. Staggering, he regained his footing and lurched towards his two wounded comrades. He managed to swing the enlisted man over his shoulder while grabbing Jackson by the collar of his jacket. Slowed by his burden, the big man stumbled towards the American line bearing the two unconscious soldiers to safety.

Jackson was removed from the field by a medivac chopper to a battalion aid station. After treatment in a military hospital in Saigon, he was air lifted to an Air Force Facility near Frankfurt Germany. His wounds were serious and there was a question if he would ever walk normally again. Still he was alive and luckier than many. His military career now in doubt, Jackson was flown back to Detroit on an extended leave where he would be reunited with his family. There he would rehab until he either fully recovered, or was medically discharged. His only regret was being unable to see Big A, his rescuer, before he was medevacked to Germany. Molina was treated for equally serious wounds and was shipped out to a medical facility in Maryland two days before Jackson. The two had crossed paths in the field hospital but both had been under sedation, and did not have a chance to speak. Both soldiers received citations from the military along with the Purple Heart and Silver Star. Jackson wrote Molina a letter thanking him for saving his life and pledging to meet him in Detroit as soon as he was able. He provided an address of his grandfather George's house in Detroit where he could be reached. He encouraged Molina to contact him there. Jackson addressed the envelope to the Detroit PO Box last listed in Molina's personnel file. Molina had no other place of residence contained in his record. Jackson did learn of Mollina's wife listed as "Beatrice" and an infant daughter, Sybil. Other than that, no information that could help him find his comrade. Jackson never knew the letter would be undelivered, lost in a helicopter crash following a missile attack on the Huey carrying it. By the time Jackson started to track down Molina in Detroit months later, his trail had grown cold. Jackson learned Molina had received psychiatric treatment for PTSD in a VA hospital in New Jersey shortly after his discharge from the Army. After that, nothing. Arturo Molina had disappeared in the underworld of his own tormented mind. Jackson had no idea how to track him down. Only the future would reveal if they would meet again.

Operation Masher was considered a tactical success with the enemy body count in excess of the total expected for the operation. The Army was pleased that the capability of the Cavalry to "find, fight, and finish" the enemy was demonstrated. The fact that enemy PAVN (North Vietnamese Troops) and VC elements returned to reoccupy that area months after the battle, intended to clear them out for good, was overlooked in all the reports. Also ignored was the fact that the battle would have to be refought in the not too distant future and would produce a similar result. More than 220 American soldiers lost their lives in the fighting along with thousands of allied and enemy soldiers, and noncombatants. Many thousands of civilians lost their homes in the violence and became refugees in their own country. That intelligence, like so much that occurred in Vietnam, was covered in a haze of ambiguity not dispelled for fifty years.

Whistle Stop 18

NOVEMBER 19, 1966

The 1967 Riot (Part 2) Julius

Julius Holloway's nimble fingers skimmed effortlessly over the gleaming piano keys. The voice of the polished ebony upright piano filled the empty night club with haunting music: *Fur Elise*. Upon completion of the Beethoven classic, Julius began playing a *Rhapsody* by Rachmaninoff, followed by a Duke Ellington composition much more recognizable to the usual patrons of this venue. He raised his voice to accompany the instrumental.

"Missed the Saturday Dance
Heard they crowded the floor
Couldn't make it without you
Don't get around much anymore"

Julius continued his medley of Ellington standards with *Satin Doll*, and *Take the A Train.*

He completed his set with an arrangement of his own, blending the chords of the classical and jazz pieces in a melodic improvisation. When he finished playing, his father Josh Holloway and sole audience for this concert applauded enthusiastically.

"Man, you really cooking"

"Thanks Dad."

Josh Holloway regularly rehearsed at the Hollow, the Paradise Valley nightspot he had owned for over twenty years. During that time an All Star assortment of great jazz and blues artists had graced the stage of this venerable space. The Temptations, Otis Redding, Curtis Mayfield, Marvin Gaye, Sam Cooke and numerous others had all performed here. The access to all this talent came from Josh's friendship with Barry Gordy whose visionary Motown record label and recording studio revolutionized American popular music. For the first time under the Motown label, the white community was introduced to the music of black performers, many of them female, like Diana Ross and Aretha Franklin, both of whom Josh knew well. The city of Detroit began to forge its national identity around the dual roles of "Motor City" as well as the incubator of the "Motown Sound". Since the riots in 1943 and the accelerating deterioration of the black neighborhoods due to urban renewal and highway construction, white patronage of the Paradise Valley nightspots had sagged but a few managed to hang on like the Hollow. Although the acoustics in this space were not as finely tuned as the Opera House or Music Hall, it was much easier and cheaper to work on his vocals during off-hours in his own night club. Josh was preparing for a performance in the opera Otello by Verdi at the Masonic Temple and his son Julius was his accompaniment this day as he ran through the arias and vocal passages of the role. Josh had fashioned a successful career straddling two very distinct musical styles, jazz and opera. Jazz paid the bills but musical theatre and opera were his passion and he enthusiastically pursued any opportunities that came his way. He remembered fondly his first big break years ago performing in Porgy and Bess in New York. That experience had propelled him to his current stardom in the burgeoning Detroit music scene, Today he was rehearsing with his son Julius, a talented musician in his own right, who seemed equally at ease in that fusion of classical and popular genres. Julius had grown up with the benefit of musical training that his father had not. From the time he was 5 years old he took piano lessons from some of the best jazz pianists in the city. By the time he had graduated from high school he was as accomplished a musician as many artists working full time in the clubs of Paradise Valley or the studios of Motown records. Moreover, he could read music, a skill his father had never quite mastered. Josh dreamed his son would follow in his footsteps but Julius had been unsettled on his career ambition through his student days. He was always a fine student and excelled in academics at St Martin De Porres High School, a coeducational Catholic School in Detroit. His attendance there led to a good natured rivalry between him and his cousin Jackson who attended the equally well regarded Cass Tech. He secretly cheered for Jackson on the football field even when his beloved Eagles had to face the Technicians on the gridiron. His cousin's acceptance at West Point had been a strong motivation for Julius and he wanted to keep pace with his accomplishments. Pursuing a career in engineering or medicine was at the top of his list when he enrolled at the University of Michigan. In the meantime, his earnings as a performer and session musician more than covered his educational expenses.

As an undergraduate at Michigan, Julius was coincidentally drawn into the counter culture movements of the era. The epicenter of this national uprising of student discontentment was in Ann Arbor. In 1960 a meeting of leftist students was convened at the University of Michigan. This gathering would eventually become the Students for a Democratic Society, or SDS, whose radical activism captured the political consciousness of so many alienated young people. The SDS was generally galvanized by the military draft and disillusionment with American imperialism. Later, as the toll from the conflict in Vietnam mounted, the organization raised a clamorous voice of opposition to the war effort. The growing Civil Rights movement was incorporated within the boundaries of SDS activism attracting many disaffected black students. It would take another decade before the Black Panther Party emerged as a separate organization with its sharp focus on the specific grievances of the black community.

Julius had a casual awareness of radical activism, but the demands of his schedule limited the time he had to get more actively involved. He was generally sympathetic to the SDS aims but not inclined to attend the endless series of organizing meetings and protests. He simply did not have the time or interest. Underlying this ambivalence was the memory of Jackson, whom he still regarded as his hero. Jackson was putting it on the line with his service in Vietnam and seemed a better role model than the student leaders. Their incessant bleating against the war seemed a self-absorbed abstraction. Besides, Julius still considered himself a patriot. He was much more in tune with Civil Rights for the black community at large than the wisdom of the Vietnam conflict. Still, he did his part through his music performing in concerts sponsored by the university at campus venues and at Ann Arbor coffee houses. While mostly offering selections of popular music and show tunes he also had a selection of protest themed music. Often these performances attracted an audience of recognized radical student leaders. At one such concert, Julius performed the Sam Cooke song "A Change is Gonna Come" which was received with great enthusiasm. As an encore, to complete his set, Julius performed the Civil Rights anthems "Blowin in the Wind" and "We Shall Overcome" as the audience sang along. Julius learned later, to his dismay, this performance had been attended by undercover agents of the Detroit office of the FBI. The obsessive J Edgar Hoover directed the bureau during this era of political paranoia and was always on the lookout for seditious conduct on the nation's campuses, particularly centered on the Civil Rights movement. Julius Holloway was being watched as a suspected sympathizer of organizations engaged in un-American activities. He was summoned to an interview at the federal building in Detroit, probing his friends and memberships in various organizations. This was especially annoying to Julius whose political sympathies were equally distant from the Communist Party as from the radical right wing John Birch Society. Julius found this interrogation to be both threatening and humiliating and he let his resentment slip which only made the tone of the agents more hostile. Their questioning became more confrontational and accusatory. Eventually, they turned their inquiry towards Julius's family. Julius learned to his horror, that his father, Josh, was a person of interest to the Bureau, being a well-known confidant of several left leaning artists. His late uncle Clem was known to have participated in the deadly 1943 race riots and as such captured the Bureau's attention. Julius found himself under a cloud of suspicion along with numerous other black entertainers whose only real agenda was a desire to perform their music, un-harassed by law enforcement.

Julius had confided his resentment to his father about the interrogation by the FBI. Josh, when he heard his son's anger sighed deeply and tears welled in his eyes. He talked about growing up in the Jim Crow South pushing a plow all day in the scorching Mississippi sun. He recalled the humiliation he endured as a Pullman porter catering to unappreciative and abusive white passengers. He spoke of how hard it was to battle the racism that closed many doors to him even before he knocked. Josh had been luckier than most in his life, but the memoires still hurt. He talked about his cousin Clem, Jackson's father, and the horrible day he was killed in the riots of 43. For one awful moment he was standing again on the Belle Isle Bridge, a farewell hymn to his cousin resonating off the sluggish current.

"This was my life and I accepted it, but I wanted so much better for you. I wanted you and Jackson to grow up where you didn't have to fight so hard just to live. Maybe your kids will see it. Maybe your kids…."

Julius understood in a flash, as if suddenly awakened. The conviction in the Declaration of Independence "all men are created equal" was only words unless written in the hearts of men. If people were unwilling or unable to internalize this principle through their own free will, then they must be chiseled indelibly into the law. From that day forward he would become a passionate advocate of the civil rights movement, and would pursue its aims through the law. As much as he loved music he passionately believed he could do more good for his community in the courtroom than the recording studio. The law was an imperfect vehicle to reach social justice. But it was the only way forward Julius could see. For the rest of his life he would dedicate himself to the law.

After graduating from the university cum laude with degrees in journalism and music, he applied to law school. His application at Michigan was rejected despite having very good academic credentials, which Julius suspected was the long malicious reach of the FBI. But through the intersession of the same congressman, who had secured appointment to West Point for Jackson, he was finally admitted. The civil rights movement had many people clamoring for change from the outside. For the rest of his career Julius Holloway would work within the law to advance the cause.

For the next three years Julius was immersed in the study of torts and contracts and the other intricacies of the law. In time his view sharpened that the laws were not necessarily made to disadvantage black citizens but to secure and maintain advantages for the white. It became obvious over time that preferential treatment under the law for whites was inherently harmful to blacks. It was equally apparent that white lawmakers would fight tirelessly to keep their advantages. The law had become more a protector of privilege for one community than a provider of justice for all citizens. This systemic bias was reflected in everything from education, to employment, housing, transportation and criminal justice which was disproportionately harsh in punishing black offenders.

Upon graduation from law school Julius became a public defender to assist clients who could not afford the services of an attorney. After a year he was given the opportunity to clerk for Thurgood Marshall, the Solicitor General of the United States who himself was only three years away from an appointment by president Johnson to the United State Supreme Court as the first black Justice. With his career just getting started Julius was already starting to his expand his contacts within the civil rights movement. He corresponded frequently with John Lewis, the 23 year chairman of the Student Non Violent Coordinating Committee (SNCC) who became a close advisor and friend. He also became familiar with Dr. King whom he met in 1963 when he appeared in Detroit on the 20th anniversary of the 1943 riots. Billed as the Walk to Freedom, King delivered a preview of what would eventually become his "I Have a Dream" oration. Two months later he would deliver similar remarks in Washington DC under the shadow of the Lincoln Memorial to a rapt audience of 250,000 lining the Mall. Dr. King was well on his way to becoming the most visible civil rights leader and one of the most hated men in the country.

Today, just as father and son, were completing their rehearsal Julius pushed back from his piano and began relating to Josh the latest news.

"Dad, I got a letter from Jackson yesterday".

Joshua was immediately concerned. He knew about his nephews wounds suffered in Vietnam.

"What did he have to say?"

"He is still recovering at the Hospital in Frankfurt Germany. Sounds like it's going to be months before they know when, or if, he will be able to return to active duty. Says he's coming home for rehab on an indefinite medical leave".

"That's big news. When does he arrive?"

"At the end of the month. Says he wants to stay with Grandpa George for a while to help him out. George needs help now getting around and Jackson reckons it would be good for both of them"

George Holloway was Jackson's grandfather and Julius's great uncle, the brother of his own grandfather Cyrus. He was a retired auto worker who still worked part time at the Rooster, a restaurant owned by Jackson's mother Althea and her husband.

After nearly five years of separation, the Holloway cousins were to meet again. It would prove to be a fateful reunion.

Whistle Stop 19

MAY 30, 1967

The 1967 Riot Judgement

Jackson Holloway's homecoming in Detroit in late 1966 found him confronting two difficult challenges. His physical rehab from his war wounds in Vietnam was slow and painful. He constantly battled frustration at the slow pace of his recovery. Although he could walk without assistance he still had a noticeable limp that slowed him and made his return to active duty in the military even more uncertain. Additionally he faced a deteriorating social climate in his community that made his already challenging life even more stressful. Tension in the black neighborhoods was simmering. The return to prosperity after the war had largely bypassed the inner city residents. Overcrowding in the depressed area of the city was becoming even more acute with 60,000 low income persons crowded into a 460 acre neighborhood. Most of these unfortunates resided in substandard-subdivided apartments. The good jobs that had supported the huge influx of migrant southern farm workers were disappearing as the Big Three automakers downsized their workforce after the boom of the war years. Increasingly the auto industry moved their operations out of Detroit into surrounding states and suburbs. Once the auto jobs began to go, more and more black Detroit residents found their personal American dream at a dead end. Urban problems of crime and poverty were on the rise. To make matters worse, the summer weather that year had been sweltering and the densely packed population suffered greatly in the oppressive heat wave. The situation was highly combustible and awaited only a match strike to ignite violence.

Jackson settled into a comfortable living arrangement with his grandfather George, now in his seventies, who had moved to Detroit from Mississippi almost 40 years before and had never left. The small house he occupied was well maintained and freshly painted and Jackson found it comfortable and convenient. George still worked part time at the Rooster, the Paradise Valley restaurant owned by Jackson's mother, Althea, and her husband Tom. Jackson himself would pitch in at the cafe on occasion as he had growing up, but his heart remained set on returning to active duty as soon as possible to resume his military career.

Jackson and his cousin Julius met frequently. Julius, as an influential attorney and a prominent voice in the Civil Rights movement, traveled frequently between Detroit and Washington where he had recently received a clerkship for the Solicitor General of the United States Thurgood Marshall. When he was in town Julius frequently performed on the piano at the Hollow, often accompanying his father Josh, a celebrated vocal artist. On those occasions the whole family would gather as special guests for the concert. The cousin's affection and mutual hero worship bound them together more closely than ever. Both determined to pursue consequential careers and make a difference in their community. They spent endless hours discussing their futures, Jackson in the military, and Julius in the law and the burgeoning civil rights movement.

Jackson spent considerable effort trying to locate Arturo Molina, the soldier under his command in Vietnam who had saved his life in Operation Masher the year before. Jackson knew Molina had been a Detroit resident before the war but his personnel records had been disappointingly incomplete about his family and place of residence. His records identified a wife named "Beatrice" and an infant daughter named "Sybil", but their last address was now a vacant building on Detroit's east side. The Detroit phone book had dozens of listings under the name "Molina" and Jackson, after a frustrating effort to contact them all, concluded that effort was futile. Unknown to Jackson, one of the Molina entries in the phone book he neglected to call was under the name Beth which had been Beatrice's nickname since childhood and the name she went by. Mother and daughter shared a flat off Mack Avenue. Jackson did not recognize the similarity of the names and gave up the effort when the connection he sought was right under his nose. If he had simply called this unrecognized phone number he would have picked up the trail of Big A.

The first real clue about Molina was discovered quite unexpectedly in a several week's old copy of local newsprint that Jackson had been browsing while seated in the waiting room of his doctor's office. The article that captured his attention concerned a local civil rights group called the *United Community League for Civic Action*, headquartered in a building nearby at the intersection of 12th Street and Claremont Avenue. Above the short article was a photograph of several people standing in front of that address. The figures in the photograph were identified as William Scott, the head of the organization, his wife Hazel, and their children, Wilma, and William Jr. Standing behind this group in the background was an unidentified figure of a very large man. Jackson could not be sure but he thought he recognized the towering figure of Arturo Molina. Could this be the one he was searching for? The woman in the photo, Wilma was identified as a secretary of the Economy Printing Company which occupied the first floor of the same building. Not mentioned in the article, the second floor housed an illegal after hours club known to the community as a "Blind Pig". The speakeasy was operated by Scott with daughter Wilma as a cook and waitress. At last Jackson had a place to start. He would visit the address to follow his first real lead.

"Blind pigs" and other afterhour's joints were common in this neighborhood of Detroit. Legal watering holes and nightclubs were mostly in suburban neighborhoods that did not welcome blacks, even if they had the means of getting there or the money to spend. Since these establishments in the inner city were unregulated they soon became the center of vice in the black neighborhoods. Gambling, drugs, and prostitution flourished in many of them and violence often broke out among patrons. The mostly all- white Detroit Police Department knew of these establishments and from time to time would raid the most notorious locations in a heavily reported effort to shut them down. But they would sprout up again like mushrooms after a heavy rain. Despite their unsavory business these establishments gave the community a place to go and congregate, socialize, get something to eat and let off some steam. As long as the joints did not make too much noise, they were frequently ignored by the police. The establishment at 9125 12th Street was relatively peaceful even hosting birthday parties, family reunions or receptions. No one seemed to be getting hurt so the establishment was left to function without harassment from the police.

When Jackson Holloway visited the address on a Friday morning he was greeted by Wilma Scott. He recognized her at once from the paper. She was a friendly 30 something woman who, when shown the photograph, did not recognize the mysterious figure standing behind her family. He may well have been simply strolling on the street and happened to be captured in the snapshot. She explained the building housed a "social club" which often drew many residents from the community not all of whom were known to her. She suggested Jackson speak with Ruby who was quickly summoned by the telephone. She arrived only minutes later down a staircase which lead to the building upper floors.

Ruby Miller Parker had worked at the Pig for five years as a bartender, occasionally supplementing her income by offering entertainment of a more personal nature in a backroom where the liquor was stored. This enterprise was sanctioned by the Scotts who received their share of the take, and Parker was discrete so there was never much fuss made over her services. Parker was wary when she first met Jackson thinking he might be an undercover vice officer. But when Jackson related his story of trying to locate his comrade from Vietnam she relaxed and provided the information Jackson sought. She recognized his image from the photo at once. Molina had been here the weekend before the snapshot was taken and Parker, though she did not mention it, had entertained him in the storeroom. She described his slow halting speech like he was very frugal how he spent his words which Jackson remembered so well about the big man. Parker told Jackson there was to be a party for two returning Vietnam vets this coming Saturday. She could not be sure but thought Molina might well be attending. It was a long shot but Jackson finally had picked up on the trail. He resolved to attend the party. Unknown to him, Molina had left town two days before on a south-bound train, the first step in a decade's long odyssey that would carry him to nearly every corner of the country. Everywhere he stopped along the way he sought the peace of mind that had been murdered in combat in Vietnam. It would be many years before Molina returned to Detroit. But for now Jackson Holloway was still hopeful for a reunion with his comrade. After all, he owed him his life.

Saturday July 22, 1967

Jackson arrived at the Pig at 11 PM. The crowd always gathered late and Jackson could see no reason to arrive early. He expected the building would be stiflingly hot and the late night hour might offer some scant relief from the heat and humidity. Or so at least Jackson hoped. In time the crowd of arrivals filled the small space to bursting with maybe 60 people talking and drinking. The open windows did let in a whisper of breeze and the electric fans sluggishly circulated the stuffy air around sweaty bodies. The noise of the party spilled into the street below and a small crowd loitered on the street smoking cigarettes and perfuming the air with the acrid aroma of marijuana, while drinking lukewarm beer from glass bottles; trying to cool off in the stifling night. Molina was not among the early arrivals but Jackson engaged the two Vietnam vets who were the honored guests at this gathering in a lively conversation. He found they had been stationed in Hue province and had participated in Operation Masher but in a different sector. The pair seemed reluctant to talk of their experiences especially to an officer, whom they feared might report them, but the more beer they drank the more outspoken they became. Jackson was not by nature a heavy drinker but the intensity of the conversation and the heavy, smoky air along with the earsplitting volume of the juke box, made the two beers he consumed go right to his head. The hours slipped away and turned into the small hours of the morning. Guests arrived and departed but no sign of Big A. But by then Jackson had become drowsy and all but forgotten the reason he was there in the first place. He must have drifted off in an unoccupied corner seated on a rickety chair with his head slumped against the wall. In his fevered dream he was once again surrounded by the night noise of Vietnam.

Jackson was jerked out his languor by the sound of screaming voices and breaking glass. His sight was blurry but he could see people hurrying to the door. There was a sound of commotion drifting up from the street below. The flashing lights atop several police cars in the street below bathed the room in a pulsing, swirling strobe of red and blue light. The atmosphere was of chaos and panic as the partygoers tried to push their way through the crushing mob fleeing the room. Jackson through the fog immediately concluded there was a raid going on. He knew in an instant this was no place he wanted to be. In the back hallway leading to the bathrooms there was a window overlooking a second story landing at the rear of the building. The open window appeared to be an escape route. As he approached the window he saw the terrified face of Ruby Miller Parker trying to overtake him to the window. On an impulse he pulled the woman before him and pushed her through the window following her close behind. From the vantage point of the landing, Jackson could see the rapidly deteriorating situation below. The noise from the crowd in the front of the building was growing louder and angrier. Jackson could make out the rush of terrified people fleeing into the shadows. A number of people were spilling into the back alley being pursued by two police officers brandishing night sticks. For a moment Jackson flashed back to his combat experience in Vietnam, only this time he was not in command and without a weapon to defend himself. Jackson seized his chance. Without a backward glance to see if Parker was safe he carefully approached the edge of the landing. Using the rain gutter and the downspout as a hand hold he swung over the edge of the landing and dropped to the alley below. He was met by an excruciating jolt of pain from his wounded leg as it absorbed the full impact of his drop. Unable to run he found himself overtaken by a burly police officer who hit him from behind. After that all went black.

When Jackson awoke he found himself still in the alley behind the speakeasy. The sky was noticeably brighter suggesting sunrise was not far away. But the more closely he surveyed his situation Jackson realized it was not the gathering dawn which illuminated the sky but the glow of fires burning all around him. Acrid smoke from the blazes choked him. The noise from the front of the building had subsided but there was the unmistakable pop of small arms fire surrounding his position. Jackson knew the next several moments were crucial if he was to escape successfully. He did his best to stand and began limping away from the noise of the fighting. It was a long slow trek but by the time the authentic glow of daybreak paled the sky he had managed to walk several blocks. There he miraculously found an early bus that was in service. He boarded the vehicle and was transported away from the riot and to the neighborhood where he resided with his grandfather George, only ten blocks away.

George met his grandson at the door with a mingled expression of panic and relief etched on his face. He informed Jackson two police officers had called on the residence just a half hour before acting on a tip that Jackson had been involved in a riot over on 12th Street. He was wanted for questioning about his role in the disturbance. Jackson had no idea how he could have been implicated in the uprising. Gradually, he worked out that either the two Vietnam vets or Ruby Miller Parker had learned his name and may have given him up to the police. Either way, he knew he might be in big trouble. He knew instinctively he would need to turn himself in to have any chance of clearing his name. Jackson immediately concluded he would need a good lawyer.

Washington DC Monday July 24, 1967

Thurgood Marshall, the Solicitor General of the United States, frowned as he read the report spread across his desk. To the side were the latest editions of the Washington Post, the New York Times, and the Detroit Free Press. Seated opposite him on the other side of the desk was Julius Holloway, his law clerk. Marshall sighed as he pushed back his chair and addressed his young aide.

"So what are we going to do about this"?

Julius replied: "The governor of Michigan has already called President Johnson. Federal troops are on their way, some are already deployed in the city. There will be tanks in the streets soon if they are not there already".

Marshall's mood darkened. He was a pioneer in the Civil Right Movement from the earliest days and been an influential advocate in the **Brown vs the Board of Education** case that overturned the sham dictum of separate but equal in American schools. He was deeply distressed by this most recent outbreak of violence.

"Tell me about your cousin" he asked.

"Jackson and I grew up together in Detroit. We were raised more like twin brothers than cousins. His Dad, my uncle, was killed in the riots of

1943. Jackson is a good, patriotic, law abiding citizen, a credit to his uniform and his race. He is totally honorable and the best man I know. He had a good reason to be at the site of the riot that night. He was there to reunite with a soldier from his platoon who had saved his life in Vietnam. The party was raided by the police around 3 AM Sunday morning. Jackson fled the scene on foot. He was identified as one of the instigators of the violence, but without evidence. We think it was a simple case of mistaken identity. Jackson turned himself in to the police immediately. He phoned me over the weekend and asked for my help. I would take a bullet for Jackson and I want to do everything I can to make this right. He is my hero and my best friend".

Marshall was moved by the sincere tribute his young clerk had presented. He had all too frequently experienced the bitter frustration of the slow pace of progress in Civil Rights. Here was an exemplary young man, a credit to his nation, let alone his race, who was under suspicion for the crime of being in the wrong place while being black.

"You need to go to Detroit and defend your cousin. I don't think the case should go to trial based on the evidence you have described. But I want to make sure that your cousin is cleared to return to the military if he wants to. We don't want the army to make an example of him. You better start at the Pentagon. I will call Bob McNamara (Secretary of Defense) and Ramsey Clark (Attorney General) and see how they want to proceed"

Based on those instructions Julius Holloway would return to Detroit to confront the reckoning of a city still in flames. He was a dedicated advocate of civil rights but this time it was more personal than that. He was fighting for justice for his own family along with his community. But it would not be easy. Jackson faced potential jeopardy in a military court martial as well as charges in a civilian criminal court. The matter would have to be handled skillfully to defend his cousin in both or either arenas. The only solution was complete vindication in both proceedings. For the sake of his cousin, Julius knew he must not fail.

Julius was frustrated by his efforts at the Pentagon. The first obstacle Julius had to navigate was the impenetrable bureaucracy of the United States military with its arcane Uniform Code of Military Justice. This Code had its earliest origins in the Continental Congress in 1777. In theory active duty military personnel could be court martialed for any crime committed while serving in the military. But one could also face criminal charges for related offenses in civilian court. What made Jackson's case tricky was, although still an active duty commissioned officer, the alleged crime occurred when Jackson was on indefinite medical leave recovering from wounds he suffered in combat. Based on his West Point background and his meritorious conduct in Vietnam, Julius presumed the military would be favorably disposed to clearing Jackson. More worrisome for the cousins was the potential charge of "conduct unbecoming an officer" which could get Jackson cashiered from the military regardless of what happened in a criminal trial in Detroit.

As he had pledged, Thurgood Marshall called Robert McNamara to discuss the case. The Secretary (DOD) was extremely interested in any issues that might impact troop morale. The implication of Jackson being a black West Point graduate was not lost on McNamara. Much of the fighting in Vietnam was being done by black draftees mostly under the command of white officers and the Secretary did not want to stir up trouble. The war in Vietnam was not going well and the government was inclined to avoid any potential for more negative publicity. Just to be certain, McNamara did confer with General William Westmoreland, the overall military commander in Vietnam. Westmoreland had personally signed off on the medals conferred on Lt. Holloway and Cprl. Molina. Westmoreland was immediately sensitive to the political issues. He recommended the lieutenant should not face a court martial unless damaging evidence was brought up in criminal proceeding. The two agreed, if the criminal court exonerated Jackson, the military would welcome him back to active duty as soon as he had recovered sufficiently. Thurgood Marshall was informed that Jackson Holloway would not face an immediate court martial, pending the results of any criminal proceedings. For the moment, Julius dropped his focus from potential military disciplinary action. Julius returned to Detroit encouraged that he was half way to his goal. Now he would have to navigate the criminal courts.

By the time Julius arrived in Detroit the following Friday, the violence had subsided. Heavily armed Federal troops and the National Guard had seized control over the neighborhoods where the worst violence had occurred. The depressing statistics were emerging and painted a grim picture. It would be months before the final toll could be assessed accurately. At least forty three people were killed, thirty three of whom were black; and 1,200 injured. Damage to property was in the $100s of millions. Over 7,200 persons were arrested, most of whom were black. The criminal trials for all those charged would begin in January of 1968. The Wayne Country Court faced the Herculean task of preparing for an avalanche of legal proceedings.

Looting, unlawful assembly, disturbing the peace, assault, curfew violations, riot, intent to kill or injure, resisting arrest, and a host of other charges were brought against the detainees. Some charges were misdemeanors and some felonious. Some of the charges would be heard in Federal court but most tried in Wayne County. Establishing conclusively the identity of the perpetrators was going to be very difficult. No doubt there were hundreds of persons innocent of criminal activity, but charged based on mistaken identity or bad timing. The court relied largely on the Detroit Police Department for evidence to support the charges.

Once the charges were determined, arraignments, bail hearings, and setting court dates all had to take place. Once again the sheer volume of these proceedings guaranteed it was going to take a long time to settle. Studies after the fact revealed the process of setting bail was harsh and arbitrary. Bail for even minor offenses such as curfew violations could be as high as $25,000 which guaranteed huge numbers of defendants would be jailed awaiting trial. Even when the bail could be met it was the practice of the court to delay release until an FBI inquiry was made to identify "outside agitators". These delays took time and resulted in terrible over-crowding in the county lock up facilities. Over a thousand black detainees were held in custody in an underground Police garage. Many other such facilities detained men, women, children, and the elderly all, in the words of one observer, "herded like cattle".

The first action Julius took was to determine where Jackson was in this overloaded system. He found the arrest record easily enough in the police precinct closest to George's house but distressingly, no other proceedings, no arraignment nor bail granted. Neither had counsel for the accused been identified. As far as Julius could tell Jackson had disappeared in the bu-reaucratic chaos of the aftermath of the riot. He immediately issued a Writ of Habeas Corpus trying to seize the initiative. Alarmingly Julius learned that no such writs were being processed in the first week after the riots. Julius began to feel panic that he might not be able to find his cousin in the chaos. Was he already too late? Had something bad happened?

Julius, through careful inquiry, was finally able to construct the se-quence of events following Jackson's surrender the morning of the riot. The situation had been so disorganized that scores of detainees were shuttled from precinct to precinct trying to find sufficient room in holding cells to lock them up. Julius learned that the last known location of his cousin was in a temporary lockup in a warehouse near the Windsor tunnel where ATF agents stored illegal items seized coming into the country from Canada. The facility was better suited for storing pallets of contraband than people. That location seemed like the best place to start looking for Jackson.

Julius produced his identification at the entrance to the warehouse. After careful inspection of his documentation Julius was admitted to the holding area. He found row after row of iron cots with thin flimsy bedding. The air was state and muggy and had the foul odor of crowded humanity. Scores of dispirited detainees were crowded into the open space. The mood in the room was sullen. Julius felt these poor wretches were in a stifling Purgatory desperate for something, anything, to happen that might break the unbearable monotony.

Julius found Jackson lying listlessly on a cot at the end of a long row close to the windows that opened on the river. The cousins embraced wordlessly for several moments. Jackson seemed thinner and in lower spirits than Julius could ever remember. But for the first moment since his confinement the cousins felt reason to hope. At the very least they would be able to initiate the proceedings to free him from this awful place.

Jackson, in compliance with Julius's writ of Habeas Corpus was brought to arraignment within a day. Julius was offered a plea deal to reduce the charges to a misdemeanor disorderly conduct offense with the promise of no additional jail time. If Jackson was willing to accept the deal he would go free immediately but with a misdemeanor criminal conviction on his record. Jackson and Julius dared not risk the potential of "conduct unbecoming an officer" charge from the military so the agreement was rejected and a plea of Not Guilty was entered. Judge George Crockett released Jackson on his own personal recognizance. Jackson and Julius made their way to Grandfather George's house for the first good meal and comfort that Jackson had experienced since the riot. Now the serious work of preparing for the trial that must clear Jackson's name would begin.

Julius believed that the willingness of the court to plead down the charge from a felony inciting a riot to a misdemeanor disorderly conduct, revealed how weak the case was against Jackson Holloway. Owing to the sheer volume of criminal proceedings it seemed likely the courts would try to plead the charges down for most of the accused and limit their incarceration to time served. Similarly, a great number of cases would result in dismissed charges for persons whose roles in the riot were either insignificant or could not be proven easily. This allowed the courts to speed through the backlog of cases. Julius felt optimistic that the charges against Jackson would be dropped but the dared not relax his efforts to make sure. His cousin's military career was at stake.

Julius devised a strategy which he felt any jury would accept. Jackson's education and meritorious service record was unassailable. The second part of the defense presentation was to corroborate that Jackson had a good and entirely sympathetic reason to be in attendance at the bar that night. Julius would prove that Jackson had every reason to believe that Arturo Molina might be present at the party. Jackson very understandably wished to reunite with the soldier who had saved his life in Vietnam. Julius was confident that a defense built on these two pillars would be successful. The obvious defect in the plan was nobody knew where to find Big A. Julius had located Ruby Miller Parker and could use her testimony that she had told Jackson about Molina's expected attendance at the party. Julius wanted more. He wanted Molina himself to appear in court and testify of his relationship with his former commanding officer. After all, Molina was a highly decorated soldier in his own right. He felt confident that this defense was his best chance for an acquittal should the case go to trial.

Julius was more thorough than his cousin in searching the Detroit phone book. He quickly discovered that "Beatrice" and "Beth" Molina were the same person and indeed the spouse of Arturo. Julius personally drove to the flat she shared with her young daughter Sybil who was just eight years old.

Beth was distraught when she learned the reason for Julius's call. She admitted she had no idea of her husband's whereabouts. She produced a handwritten letter from him detailing his fears about his dangerous mental state and his desire to protect his wife and child by fleeing the city. It was clear there would be no way to produce Arturo as a witness at trial. Beth tearfully begged Julius to help find her husband and to assure him his family wanted him home. Julius produced a sheet of notebook paper and wrote Grandpa George Holloway's name, address, and phone number on it to give to Beth. If she needed to reach him, this was the best way. Both he and Jackson might be difficult to track. George was a reliable and readily accessible contact to relay information to the cousins. He promised he would do whatever he could to help Beth find her husband.

Julius made one final effort to get the charges dropped against Jackson and to keep the matter from going to trial. He contacted Thurgood Marshall who agreed to his suggestion. The following letter was delivered to Judge George Crockett the next week.

To the Honorable George Crockett
Judge of the Recorders Court

First Lieutenant Jackson Holloway is a decorated Vietnam veteran, a West Point graduate and a platoon commander in Vietnam. He was awarded a Purple Heart and Silver Star for valor in Operation Masher where he risked his life to rescue one of the troops in his command. In the same engagement, a soldier under his command saved Lt. Holloway's life and was similarly decorated. Lt. Holloway was attending a party at an illegal after hour's club in Detroit where he resides on a temporary medical leave to rehabilitate his wounds. He hoped to reunite with the soldier who saved his life who Holloway believed would be in attendance. The party was raided by the police in the early hours of Sunday morning which sparked the riot. Lt. Holloway fled the scene on foot. Lt. Holloway committed no crimes that anyone present has been able to substantiate. He was identified as one of the instigators of the violence, by a witness who later recanted her testimony. Lt. Holloway's father was killed in the Detroit riots in 1943. Lt. Holloway turned himself in to the police immediately. It is the opinion of the signers that the case against Lt Holloway does not merit criminal charges. We believe that the pursuit of better relations between white and black soldiers is beneficial to the military and the pursuit of equal justice for all its citizens is in the country's best interest. We the undersigned respectfully request Lt. Holloway be cleared of all charges so that he may resume his military career.

The letter was signed by Robert McNamara, Secretary of Defense, Ramsey Clark, Attorney General, William Westmoreland, Field Commander in Vietnam, and Thurgood Marshall Solicitor General of the United States.

Judge Crockett officially dropped the charges against Jackson Holloway the very day he received the letter. In the chaotic aftermath of the riots the Justice Department had the nearly impossible task of dispensing justice to a completely unjust situation. The black community had been treated dreadfully by the law during their long, sad residency in Detroit. Tragically, blacks were often treated as if they had brought it on themselves; somehow to blame for their own misery. Justice demanded that from time to time the fine points of the law be disregarded in favor of what was simply right.

The Detroit race riots of 1967 sparked an accelerated decline in the population and prosperity of Detroit. But for Julius and Jackson Holloway the uprising was merely an introduction to the next phase of their careers. Many battles had yet to be fought but for the moment both cousins enjoyed the satisfying yet fleeting experience of vindication.

Whistle Stop 20

EPILOGUE (PART 1) 1969

The 1967 Riot

While Jackson Holloway's health and mobility improved in 1968, his Grandfather George was declining. George had always been a thoughtful contemplative man who drew great comfort from his Bible. Now, as he faced the ending of his days, he would sit for hours seeking solace in the Scriptures. More and more his mind focused on things in the past, the hardscrabble childhood in Mississippi and the tough years he had spent in the unwelcoming regimentation of factory life. He spoke frequently of his son Clem, laid to rest here in Detroit, and Clem's mother Alice, buried back home in Mound Bayou. As the weeks passed, his energy ebbed noticeably and he was less and less seen at the Rooster, performing his daily routine. Jackson knew the reckoning would come soon enough with his expected return to the military. Once Jackson received his orders, George would be alone in the small house he had lived in for years. Julius would always be nearby but had his own life, a growing family, and a career to attend to. Althea, Clem's widow and her husband Tom would gladly take George in, but he did not want that. His house contained all his memories, good and bad, from 40 years and he could not bear to leave it.

Finally, Jackson received his orders. He would not be returning to Vietnam. Instead he would be stationed in eastern Bavaria in Grafenwohr, a remote base that confronted the threat from the Soviets and their Warsaw Pact clients behind the nearby Iron Curtain. Jackson was to be an intelligence officer helping to maintain a high level of military readiness. Graf was sometimes referred to as the tip of the spear. If the Soviet bear came over the wall it would be the soldiers manning this lonely outpost who would be first to challenge him. Jackson had only a month before he had to report. George had taken the news of his grandson's departure placidly but he did have one request to make of his family. He assembled the clan at the Rooster the next night to make known his wishes.

"I have lived here in Detroit for 40 years but this never felt like home. I want you all when I am gone, to return Clem and me to Mound Bayou to be buried at home in the churchyard of Brother Franklin's church. I want to rest next to my wife Alice, and Cyrus and his family when their time comes. Jackson, I want you to promise me you won't come all the way home from Germany to be at my funeral. When you return to the States please leave flowers on our graves. That will be enough".

The family tearfully agreed to this request but all harbored the hope this unhappy commitment would not need to be fulfilled any time soon. But George knew better. Barely a week later, three weeks before Jackson was scheduled to leave the country George Holloway passed peacefully with his entire family on hand to bid him farewell.

Josh Holloway, head of the Detroit clan, arranged for the remains of George and Clem to be transported back to Mississippi accompanied by all the local Holloway family. He had decided that the railroad would provide the appropriate transport. He himself had ridden these same rails to freedom so many years before and it seemed fitting the cortege should complete the circuit. This morning, as his family gathered in Michigan Central, he noticed how much the station had changed over the years. The waiting room was still clean and functional but missing the bustling crowds who used to fill the terminal. He pondered the rapid passing of time and the deep symbolism of the odyssey upon which he was embarking. Without dwelling on it, he knew he was unlikely to occupy this space again. He seldom ventured out of the state anymore and when he did travel to attend a musical performance, he usually would fly or drive. So many important events in his life had occurred here in the railroad station and now his memory flooded, recalling all these milestones. He struggled to say goodbye to a place and time receding into the past. At the assigned hour the train left the station; Josh Holloway's final departure from Michigan Central Station. The mournful journey would trace the bends of the Great River back to the south land, the country of his family's birth, which had so cruelly expelled these, their native sons, but in whose welcoming soil the refugees would find a final homecoming.

Whistle Stop 21

OCTOBER 20, 1944

The Game

T he ball bounced off the turf and rebounded perfectly. John Brogan, the Boys Town Dodgers star player and jack of all trades, skillfully timed his kick to impact the ball at just the right spot on its surface. The plunking noise, similar to the deep hollow thump of slapping a watermelon, announced the kick was true. It sailed in a beautiful arc 40 yards toward the goalposts. It split the uprights with plenty of distance to spare. Executing a successful drop kick was not easy. The elliptical shape of the ball meant its bounce off the ground was never reliably perfect. Dozens of small things could go wrong dooming the result. John Brogan,

Boys Town varsity fullback, was an expert at the seldom attempted play. Skip Palrang, the Boys Town coach, kept it in the playbook as a just in case gambit. One of these days that play would be exactly what was needed in a game. When that moment came, Palrang intended to be ready. That pretty much summed up his approach to coaching. Prepare for anything because sooner or later, anything will happen.

"Nice kick Johnny" he shouted.

He turned to Father Flanagan at his side and proclaimed the obvious.

"Man, that kid can kick a football!" the coach enthused.

"He certainly can" the priest agreed.

The two men were overseeing the final practice before the squad embarked on a long road trip. The Boys Town varsity was boarding a train in Omaha the next morning that would carry them half way across the country to Michigan. Their opponent in the upcoming game was the power house Shamrocks of Detroit Catholic Central. Although this year's Shamrocks squad was struggling through an uncharacteristically tough season, they still were regarded as the best program in Michigan. Their reign as Detroit City Champions went back to 1938. The *Detroit Free Press* recently published a report detailing how exacting their methods were to locate and develop talent. The effort began in elementary school and continued until a player arrived at the varsity level years later. The result was a deep stable of very talented players. The team was so successful that it often drew huge crowds to very large stadiums. Tough and experienced, the Detroit team was going to be hard to beat especially in front of their home town fans.

Flanagan scanned the Shamrocks roster printed in the newspaper. He noted that at nearly every position, the Detroit players were bigger than his lads, especially in the all-important line positions. He was not disturbed. His players were frequently undersized but they were fleet footed to a man. Besides, his student body, made up of homeless boys, had faced greater obstacles in their young lives than any of their opponents. Their advantage was in their character and no team could compete with that.

They played with great courage and determination that most of the time produced victories. This year's record was unblemished as they prepared for Catholic Central. Pound for pound, they were thought by many to be the best high school team in the country. Now they would face a challenge that could prove the claim.

The fact that Boys Town was willing to travel such a long way for a mere football game says a lot about the vision of their founder Edward Flanagan. Born in Ireland, he immigrated to America as a youngster in 1904. After ordination to the priesthood, a passion emerged that would become his life's mission. It was summed up by his ardent and often asserted belief that there was no such thing as a bad boy. He believed errant youngsters deserved a second chance instead of a reform school sentence. Despite initial opposition from his superiors he finally succeeded in establishing Boy's Town as a facility for homeless and delinquent boys at a location near Omaha. He set about the great work of turning throw-away youngsters into successful men. He would rehabilitate those who required it while providing a good education for all.

Flanagan believed that athletics were essential to develop confidence, self-esteem and physical fitness for his charges. So he set out to build a successful sports program. He was especially fond of football. He compared it to a sermon whose powerful life's lessons were just the sort of instruction boys needed. His plans were frustrated though by his difficulty scheduling games close to home. Many of the area public schools did not want to schedule the upstart and racially integrated Boys Town teams. Virtually no one wanted to play in their inadequate facilities. Flanagan saw quickly that if he wanted to compete with the best, he would have to go to them. In 1944 an opportunity presented itself. Matching the powerful Shamrocks team against the Boys Town eleven in an intersectional match would produce a game with great appeal as a fund raiser to benefit both schools. The two schools agreed and the game was set. The next day would begin their journey to an epic clash, the best team in Michigan vs the best team in the country.

The train ride was long and tiresome through the great prairie lands of the American Midwest. Flanagan clutched his rosary beads and tried to stay awake as the mundane miles rolled past his window, as repetitive as the decades of the rosary he recited to himself. He was a pious man but he always had trouble keeping his mind from wandering during the rosary. He tried but inevitably lost concentration. Somehow he was sure Our Lady did not hold it against him. Today he was distracted by other more earth bound concerns. Would his boys be up to the task confronting them? Would they present themselves as outstanding representatives of their schools values and traditions? Winning the game was important but secondary to the greater goal of becoming better citizens. Finally he succumbed to the monotony and he fell asleep with his head rolling uncomfortably on his shoulders. Meanwhile, Coach Palrang, who was not a praying man, was drawing up plays in his head while keeping watch over his young charges. Palrang knew the Shamrocks ran an offense patterned after Notre Dame's vaunted "box formation". His own team favored an offense resembling the Chicago Bears potent single wing. He believed that when facing superior talent detailed preparation was the great equalizer. So he sifted through every detail to find an edge he could exploit. He would be ready. As their coach schemed, the boys kept busy reading and horsing around. Time enough for them to get serious when they got to Detroit.

When the train finally arrived at Michigan Central, the team was greeted on the platform by a delegation from Catholic Central. Leading the welcoming committee were Father James Martin, athletic director and Alex Chesney, head coach along with the Catholic Central marching band, 80 members strong, to greet their rivals. The Boys Town contingent was impressed by the warmth of the reception and its hospitality, exceeding the requirements of sportsmanship. This was motivated in part by the excitement of the upcoming game. Sportswriters from throughout the region were present to cover the contest and it was obviously considered an important event. In addition to that, Father Flanagan himself was a dignitary whose visit merited the fanfare such a famous and beloved person deserved.

Boy's Town and its illustrious founder were world famous, especially since the 1938 film earned Spencer Tracy a Best Actor Oscar for his portrayal of Father Flanagan in the Hollywood version of the story.

Leaving the station the assembly proceeded by bus to the downtown Book Cadillac Hotel for a welcoming breakfast for both teams. This gave the visitors their first sight of their rival Shamrocks. They were all big kids and looked like grown men. John Brogan felt a flicker of apprehension and a nagging doubt. Can we play with these guys? The breakfast featured remarks from several local dignitaries, mostly CC old grads. But the gathering was cordial with none of the taunting trash talk of latter years. The word "swagger" was not yet acceptable as a substitute for "confidence". Both teams knew they were good but the standards of the time discouraged boasting about it. The administrations of both schools worked hard to instill the value of sportsmanship. Simpler times indeed.

After the breakfast, the two teams separated. The Nebraska squad was conducted on a tour of the city which concluded with a visit to the Ford Rotunda. Most of the boys were from small towns and rural backwaters. The sights and sounds of Detroit, a city so much bigger than Omaha, were overwhelming. Everywhere the bustle of the arsenal of democracy was on display. Again the twinge of self-doubt plucked at their hearts. Some began to fear they were in over their heads. Only Father Flanagan and Coach Palrang seemed unfazed. Their calm demeanor seemed to settle the team.

Game day: October 22, 1944

The two teams marched around Briggs Stadium along Michigan Avenue in an impromptu parade before entering the stadium. Excited onlookers cheered. If the Nebraskans felt any lingering anxiety it was dispelled by the sight of 43,000 fans cheering lustily as the teams took the field. The rush of adrenaline and testosterone flooded the blood vessels of both teams until it was nearly impossible to restrain them. The mayhem could be delayed only long enough for a ceremonial kickoff performed by Fathers Flanagan and Martin representing the two schools. Flanagan's kick soared 35 yards which drew a roar of approval from the huge crowd. Photographers stood by to capture this moment. This was followed by the actual kickoff and the game was underway.

As expected, the contest was a physical hard hitting affair casting the superior speed of Boy's Town against the greater size of the Shamrocks. CC drew first blood early in the game after Boys Town fumbled near mid field. The Shamrocks took the turnover and uncorked two consecutive long runs that found the end zone. Late in the first quarter the Dodgers returned the favor after a brilliant defensive stand produced a blocked punt recovered by Boys Town at the Catholic Central four yard line. On the first play of the seconds quarter Rusty Vigil took it in for the Dodgers to tie the game at seven. The score remained knotted until after halftime when Boys Town's ace, John Brogan hauled in a beautiful pass and took it in for the go ahead score. For the remainder of the third quarter and deep into the fourth the Dodgers held their lead. The air was electric with tension. Could the Shamrocks come back and pull this one out? They had dominated most of the statistics except the only one that mattered. But it was clear that the undersized Nebraskans were exhausted and holding on by the skin of their teeth. Now it was down to a simple test of wills. Who would prevail? With about three minutes remaining the Shamrocks had time for one last drive to try and save the game.

The Shamrocks began the drive at midfield but immediately drew a five yard penalty moving them backwards into their own territory. Two consecutive completions from CCs Joe Miglio to 6'3" all stater Bill Whitkin advanced the ball to the Boys Town 30. But the next three CC passes fell harmlessly incomplete brining up 4th down for the Shamrocks. Most of the partisan crowd groaned but the Boys Town faithful were on their feet screaming wildly.

At moments such these, indelible memories are made. On 4th down Miglio threw a perfect strike hauled in by Whitkin good for 28 yards and a CC first down and goal to go from the two with 34 seconds to play. Johnny

McMahon plunged through the line on the next play for the CC score. Now it came down to the all-important extra point. CC's attempted run was stopped short causing a wild eruption of emotion from the Boys Town faithful. This outburst of elation quickly turned to anguished disbelief. The referee had signaled off sides against the Dodgers. CC would get a second chance. The exhausted Nebraskans gave a heroic but futile effort to stop CC but they had nothing left. The successful extra point sealed the tie as the gun sounded only a moment later. The best against the best finished knotted at 14.

Postscript

The Boys Town team, some of them in tears after the spoilage of their perfect season, was greeted in the locker room by Father Flanagan who congratulated each of them heartily. Moments later the entire Shamrock squad filed into the visitors' locker room to shake hands with their opponents in a gesture of sportsmanship.

Boys Town would have its revenge in 1945 beating CC 14-12 in the second game of the series. In 1947 Boys Town would prevail again.

The thrilling games between CC and Boys Town started the annual tradition of Boys Bowl, conducted each year at Catholic Central pitting the Shamrocks against the toughest competition from the Catholic School League. Each year it is a weekend long celebration with many traditional events for students and alumni.

"Here's to the famous games whose memories still quicken
the pulse
As fresh and evergreen as youth itself
Yet tinted with age and certified by tradition
Fleet-footed shadows are running still, breaking free
As elusive from time as once from defenders
And in that secret place where memory lives
The old are made young again"

Whistle Stop 22

SEPTEMBER 6, 1964

The Concert

Marcia Koning, aged 18, tried to make herself comfortable sitting cross legged on the hard floor of Olympia Stadium. Since she was likely going to be here awhile she thought she might as well get some schoolwork done. She had a book perched in her lap, an introduction to Freud and psychoanalysis. Even in a more comfortable setting with less swirling commotion she would have found the effort to concentrate very difficult. Here she merely went through the motions. She was a freshman at Michigan State University, intending to major in psychology. She took her studies seriously but on this day was distracted by an event of unusual excitement. Like everyone else in the long queue, she was waiting for the opening of the ticket office. That space beckoned like Eldorado at the head of the long line. What could have prompted so many, mostly teenage girls, to endure such crowded confines on this rainy April morning? Nothing less than the opening of ticket sales in just a few short hours, for the Beatles first concerts in Detroit. The lads from Liverpool would be playing two shows at the Olympia on the Sunday before Labor Day, five months away. The afternoon concert would begin at 2 PM and the evening concert at 7 PM. For most of the adolescent female population of the city being in line to purchase a ticket was an event that totally justified skipping school.

Marcia being older, and a college student, viewed the animation of the high school and junior high girls with some amusement. She liked to think of herself as mature and largely unfazed by the frenzy surrounding her. Even so, she was determined to be among the first to acquire precious tickets for the show. She made certain that she arrived early to get a good spot in line. Judging from the crowd, most of the other girls had the same plan. She was four hours into her wait and still fairly far back in line. She rationalized her attendance at the concert would be an educational experience. She intended to observe the hysterical behavior of so many adoring fans from a psychological point of view. She even thought she would write a paper about the experience for one of her classes. But deep inside, she harbored the fantasy of meeting George Harrison (her favorite Beatle) in person and maybe getting an autograph, or possibly securing a date. Her heart raced at the thought of it.

Marcia had already planned the weekend with her parents. They arranged for the short train ride from her native Saginaw to Detroit, the Saturday before the concert. In Detroit she could stay overnight with her best friend and MSU classmate, Barbara Comstock, who lived in Indian Village and would accompany her to the concert. Marcia had enough money in her pocket to pay for the two tickets. Still months away, the anticipation was almost overpowering. Only early spring, but she was already looking ahead to the end of summer. With her mind filled with so many pleasant thoughts she forgot all about Freud. He could wait. For now, she whiled away the hours until she, at last, reached the head of the line. There she claimed her treasure. Now she faced months of impatiently waiting.

Finally the morning of departure arrived and Marcia found herself in a jammed packed rail car for the short 40 minute train ride to Michigan Central. Among the passengers were a large group of teenage girls obviously on the same journey as Marcia. Upon arrival at the station, Marcia met Barbara, waiting for her on the platform. The Beatles would arrive at the airport just after midnight tonight. She shared the breathtaking news that the Beatles would then proceed by motorcade to the Book Cadillac Hotel. Although this intelligence was unsubstantiated, it was an entirely believable rumor. The story had been passed among a few fans under strictest confidence not to tell anyone. So, naturally the whole town was buzzing with the news. Barbara herself had called the hotel to verify the report. She was told emphatically that the Beatles were NOT staying there but Barbara suspected a deception. In reality the management of the hotel was disappointed they were not hosting the Beatles. It was an event of great interest and would have created tremendous publicity. As a consolation prize they had the arrival of another important party to prepare for. Lyndon Johnson, the President of the United States, was scheduled to arrive at the Book Cadillac the morning after the concert to attend a reception kicking off his campaign for the 1964 election. To most of the concert goers this was an irrelevant coincidence. Generally the crowd at the concert was too young to vote and indifferent to politics. After all, Presidents come and go, but there was only one Fab Four.

Leaving the station, the girls proceeded to a downtown Denny's diner for breakfast and to plan the weekend. Even at that late arrival hour, there would be a large crowd at the airport to welcome the band. The girls decided to pass on that event in favor of proceeding directly to the hotel to witness the group's arrival downtown. Their chances of a close encounter there were better. They would remain in vigil before the hotel as long as their endurance permitted.

After breakfast the girls proceeded to Barbara's home in Indian Village. They spent the warm afternoon playing tennis and speculating about the day's events. Around 4:30 Barbara received a phone call from one of her friends whose father was a police officer. As it happened he would be part of the Beatles escort. The caller had new intelligence to share. The Beatles were not staying at the Book Cadillac downtown, but at the nearby Whittier only a few short blocks from Barbara's home in Indian Village. This location was known for its spacious apartment style lodging and stunning views over the Detroit River. This change in plans perfectly suited the two girls. They would proceed to the hotel by 10 PM. There they would wait until the action started. Even with the secrecy of the band's arrival it was expected there would be huge crowd present. With luck they would get several close-up views of their idols in the wee hours of the morning. Maybe, if they were extremely lucky, even a chance to speak with them. Marcia grew tongue tied at the mere thought of such an encounter.

The hour arrived and the friends found themselves standing in a crush of excited spectators near the front entrance to the Whittier. Approximately an hour after the Beatles arrival at the airport, a phalanx of police cars announced the approach of the band. The local media was on hand to cover the event. They attempted to interview the fans for their reaction but mostly elicited screams of sheer excitement. Two brand new shiny Lincoln Town Cars pulled up to the entrance. The first one out of the lead car was Ringo and the explosion of noise that greeted him seemed to startle him. He looked momentarily intimidated by the commotion. He seemed disheveled as if he has been dozing in the car. After all it was only a matter of a few short hours ago they were on stage in Chicago followed by a frantic rush to the airport and a turbulent late night flight to Detroit. Such was a day in the life of the Beatles. Fame had its rewards but it certainly had a price as well. He hesitated for a moment then broke into a broad grin. He tossed a wave at the crowd and stepped aside to allow his mates to exit the vehicles. One by one they stepped out on to the street, first John, followed by George, then Paul. The reaction from the crowd was pure bedlam. Beaming, the group paused momentarily to allow the photographers to take their pictures then retreated through the entrance to the lobby beyond. The sighting was barely more than a glimpse, but the crowd reacted as if they had witnessed a divine vision. Many of the girls were weeping hysterically and had to be supported lest they faint in the street. Marcia was in ecstasy. Already their plan had been rewarded. They had consumed a large slice of cake. Now they were hungry for the icing. They settled in for a long night of watchfulness.

The girls were rewarded again for their patience. By 2 AM only a handful of bystanders remained. Then unexpectedly, almost like a luminous mirage, the unmistakable figure of George Harrison appeared outside the entrance door. He held a package of cigarettes and had clearly stepped outside into the fresh air to have a smoke. He, like Ringo, looked tired. Clearly it took a lot of stamina, even for a young person, to be a rock star. The two friends approached him reverently as if approaching a deity. Harrison flashed a warm smile and spoke in his charming unmistakable Liverpool accent.

"Hello Luv. Are you coming to see the show?"

The girls stammered that they were. They gushed incoherent adulation which Harrison accepted in good grace. He then asked politely.

"Would you like an autograph?"

Marcia produced her notebook and a pen. Harrison asked.

"What's your name, luv?"

Harrison scrawled on the page. To Marcia, September 6, 1964 George Harrison.

He performed the same service for Barbara who nearly fainted in the street. Marcia was seized by an irresistible urge. She stretched to her full height and kissed the Beatle on his cheek. He smiled faintly, completely accustomed to such impulsive affection.

"Gotta go now, Thanks for coming."

Without another word he crushed his cigarette butt underfoot, turned and entered the hotel.

The girls remained through most of the night hoping for another encounter. Finally as the pale light of dawn was breaking over the city, they gave up exhausted. They returned to Indian Village for a bit of rest and nourishment. By 10:00 AM they returned to the Whittier to resume their watch. The Beatles checked out of the hotel and proceeded to the Olympia by motorcade in the early afternoon. To avoid the gathering crowds the band had left from an inconspicuous side entrance. The girls did not spot their idols but did see the motorcade speed away.

The two friends now had several hours to recuperate at Barbara's house. By now they were running on pure adrenaline, consumed by the exhaustion and euphoria. At 5:30 PM, they boarded a charter bus which delivered them to the Olympia for the evening concert.

The show itself was a blur. The warm up acts were excellent and generated more than polite enthusiasm. But there was no mistaking that these acts were appetizers to a greatly anticipated main course. Once the Beatles took the stage, the screaming never stopped during their 25 minute set. Marcia could barely hear the music over the din, but didn't really care. Just being there was amazing enough. After the show, the band once again raced back to the airport for another late night flight to Toronto and the continuation of their tour. Detroit, suddenly dispossessed of its heroes, had basked in the glow of their presence for a mere 24 hours.

For Marcia and Barbara, both of whom would have long happy lives, this was an experience of unusual importance. They reminisced about it constantly for many years to come. Nothing short of the births of their children would match the sheer undiluted joy of that encounter. For the briefest of moments their lives intersected with an artist whose global fame and historical significance, made him beloved by millions. Both of them would weep inconsolably at the news of Harrisons passing from cancer at the age of 58 in 2001. He would remain forever a cherished icon of their long lost youth.

Postscript

Marcia spent the night of the concert with Barbara at her home in Indian Village. She awoke still awash with the afterglow of the previous night's magic. Barbara drove her friend to Michigan Central in midmorning to catch her train back to Saginaw. They were delayed by the traffic congestion caused by the Presidential motorcade passing along Michigan Avenue. They could see the unmistakable jowly profile of Lyndon Baines Johnson through the window of his limousine. He gave a wave in their general direction causing Marcia to remark wistfully to her friend:

"I can't believe I kissed George Harrison. I wonder if I'll ever see him again"

Whistle Stop 23

OCTOBER 31, 1926

The Magician

If there was one thing Eric Weiss truly craved it was the reaction his unusual occupation inspired. He relished the changing expressions on the faces of mystified audiences in the sold out venues where he performed. It usually started as a countenance of extreme concentration. The crowd was studying every movement that might betray the secret of the miracle being observed. It rapidly changed to an aspect of utter disbelief as the trim athletic little man had apparently suspended the laws of nature. Finally, the audience displayed facial expressions of sheer delighted confusion followed by thunderous applause. Written on the faces of the entire assembly the burning question: How in the world did he do that? Such were the range of emotions that Harry Houdini commanded each time he took the stage. That was what Houdini lived for.

He had started his career in vaudeville but by 1926 was acclaimed as of the greatest entertainers of the era which featured luminaries like Rudolf Valentino and the redoubtable Babe Ruth. Such fame brought him great wealth and universal acclaim. He etched his name indelibly into the pantheon of immortal characters whose names became synonymous with their craft. To the entire world the name Houdini meant MAGIC.

Houdini discovered early in his career that the audience was a willing accomplice to this trickery. They WANTED to be fooled. Despite their apparent effort to understand the hoax, they preferred to be dumbfounded. The audience wanted to believe they were witnessing magic. A sophisticated viewer might know intuitively that magic was not real, but that would spoil the fun. If they could easily explain how Houdini performed his marvels they would cease to be interested in him. Houdini understood that and went about astounding his audience with incredibly skilled, but completely explainable illusions.

He had begun his career with the conventional array of sleight of hand, card tricks and disappearing illusions that were the magician's stock in trade. It was only when he discovered his talent for escaping from restraints like hand cuffs, straight jackets, and rope binding that he found the formula for great success and his lasting legacy. He would forever be renowned as the foremost escape artist in the world, a man who could not be shackled or imprisoned. Many of these escapes were accomplished by Houdini's incredible physical skills. He had the ability to expand and contract his wrists so that he could slip out of handcuffs. He was said to be able to dislocate his shoulders so that no straight jacket could hold him. His most outrageous claim was that he was so flexible and well balanced; he could stand on a chair and bend over to pick up a needle off the floor with his eyelids. Houdini did not discourage these stories. He was enough of a showman to appreciate the publicity. Less frequently told were the non-magical devices

Houdini would sometimes use to accomplish his marvels. A concealed key or lengths of picklock wire were essential to facilitate some of his escapes.

Houdini's escapes grew progressively more difficult and dangerous. The audiences were captivated by seeing the magician cheat death and Houdini was quick to oblige. He would be sealed in barrels; one filled with beer as a nod to an audience of brewers; be submerged in a variety of containers, or suspended from a crane by a rope while clothed in a straight jacket. He was buried in 6 feet of earth and claimed afterward the ordeal nearly killed him. He famously was tossed hang cuffed off the Belle Isle Bridge into the frigid waters of the Detroit River only too emerge shivering but unharmed. Once when a dead whale washed ashore in Boston Harbor he proposed to escape from its belly mimicking Jonah's famous feet. But his most notorious escape was from a flooded glass chamber suspended upside down by manacles on his ankles. Called the Chinese Water Torture Cell, Houdini performed it many times for fascinated and terrified audiences. Just when the crowd was sure that Houdini must drown, he would reappear behind a concealing screen perfectly safe.

On a late October evening in 1926, Houdini sat in his dressing room in Montreal's Princess Theater rehabbing a broken ankle he had suffered in an earlier performance. As a publicity stunt, he had often bragged his abdomen was so firm he could withstand any physical blows to his gut. Sadly, a young man, Jocelyn Gordon Whitehead, decided to test that claim. After asking for permission the young man launched a flurry of violent punches to the stomach which left Houdini wincing in pain. It was never clear whether the attack caused the rupture of his appendix or simply inflicted great pain but either way, Houdini was in deep distress. He refused medical attention and insisted on remaining on his schedule.

He was bound by train for Detroit the next day to begin a series of performances at the Garrick Theater. His overnight ride on the jolting train was excruciating. He suffered from nausea and lightheadedness and could not manage to sleep. When he arrived at Michigan Central he was feeling only slightly better but did fall into a fitful sleep when he reached his hotel.

October 24, Houdini insisted on performing his scheduled show at the Garrick Theater even though he was burning with a fever of 104 degrees. Many in the audience that night remembered he seemed off his game, but still struggled mightily to complete his performance. He collapsed midway through the show but was revived and attempted to continue. Once it was concluded there was something seriously wrong he was rushed to nearby Grace Hospital and diagnosed with acute peritonitis, a deadly infection from his ruptured appendix. He survived emergency surgery but finally succumbed the following Sunday; fittingly enough for one who was an outspoken critic of fake spiritualists, on Halloween night. It was reported that on the 10th anniversary of his death a séance failed in their effort to contact Houdini beyond the grave. Whatever remaining secrets of his life would continue unrevealed, secure in a vault of silence even he could not escape. His legacy as the greatest magician of all time is secure.

Whistle Stop 24

JANUARY 13, 1983

The Commuter

The alarm clock on the bedside table delivered the bad news: 6 AM, time to get up. Ron cursed under his breath. The darkness outside his bedroom window gave no clue as to the time of day. He had to depend on the announcement from his alarm clock to get his temporal bearings. He had tried setting the clock radio to awaken to music but found that was not always persuasive enough to coax him out of bed. So he selected a shrill, insistent tone, unpleasant on the ears, but impossible to ignore. He hated having his dreams invaded so rudely each morning, but at least the auditory assault would sufficiently awaken him to withstand the temptation of his warm bed to push the snooze button. He would rise with ample time to shave, shower, and gulp down a cup on the way out the door, to catch the 7:15 Amtrak train to Detroit.

Ron lived in Ann Arbor. He commuted every work day to downtown Detroit where he worked for the Ford Motor Company in the gleaming 300 tower of the Renaissance Center. Being averse to the daily hour long drive in heavy traffic he sought alternatives for his commute. Carpooling was a little too dependent on the schedules of other and was subject to the same traffic congestion as driving alone. His analytical mind quickly concluded that Amtrak was a viable option to get downtown each morning. The savings per mile were not substantial but the idea of never having to drive his own car in rush hour traffic was appealing. He had started the railroad commute on a trial basis. Now he was sold on the idea. He would take the train into the city most mornings.

The inbound 50 minute ride made a single stop in Dearborn before arrival at MCS. Just enough time to scan the headlines, or doze. He often reviewed his schedule for the day, organizing his required tasks. On some occasions he would converse with his fellow commuters, several of whom he got to know quite well. Upon arrival in Detroit he would board a bus for the Renaissance Center to report to work by 8:20 AM. If the train was behind schedule his late arrival at the office was sure to be noticed by his bosses. But Ron remained unperturbed by criticism.

On those occasions when Ron had a project deadline approaching or a meeting late in the day, he would drive himself in, allowing him to stay later. But he tried to avoid that. His bosses sometimes groused that a management employee needed to be present after the normal work day. "Casual overtime" was the norm for ambitious employees seeking promotion. But Ron was unmoved by the implicit threat. As a child of the 60s he was not consumed with his career. He was not about to give in to the unreasonable expectations of corporate culture just to climb the ladder. So at 4:50 PM each day he would leave the office to catch the 5:45 PM train home. He would board the bus outside the Renaissance Center by 5:01 PM and be delivered to Michigan Central with 15 minutes to spare. Ample time if traffic was not unexpectedly heavy. But he was used to cutting it close. One snowy day in December he had missed his connection and had to wait for the next train leaving at 8:15 PM. That was annoying but preferable to a $50 cab fare to Ann Arbor. All the way home, his mind seethed with the thought of the ruined supper awaiting him. Such were the hidden costs of commuting by train.

Ron made this twice a day migration between Ann Arbor and Detroit hundreds of times, investing thousands of hours of his life in the journey. For him, the trip was purely a practical part of his routine. He seldom stopped to think about the countless millions who had shared this space. For him, as with most commuters, Michigan Central Station marked where the workday began and ended, an arrangement of convenience, a simple, logistical choice, nothing more. Even so, when the station closed in1988 Ron did feel a pang of emotion, a sense of loss that he found hard to express. He felt a vague, inexpressible longing for a time from his own past, now gone forever. The daily circuit between work and home had been the metronome keeping time for his days for over a decade. Its measured pulse clicked off the milestones of a career and a life that had passed, along with the weary miles, too quickly.

Whistle Stop 25

NOVEMBER 13, 2009

The Quest

Louis Ochoa was well known among the homeless in Detroit. He was known simply as Packo, no other first or last name. Social workers and charitable agencies all knew him. People who lived on the street knew him. Even the cops would occasionally stop the old man and ask how he was getting on. He was regular at overnight shelters during winter when living outside was impossible. On most days when conditions allowed he could be seen loitering in public places like the bus depot or the library, snatching sleep wherever he could. He was a regular customer of the Saturday morning charity ministry in Cass Corridor where he patiently waited in line hoping for his favorite bologna sandwiches. He knew where and when he could procure clothing and toiletries donated by churches throughout the city. He was able on occasion to enjoy the blissful cleansing of a shower. Even though friendships were rare in the dog-eat-dog world of street life, he had a wide circle of acquaintances with whom he co-existed peacefully. He seemed to have figured out how to survive in a world of appalling danger, filth, degradation and brutality where life expectancy was measured in months, not years. In a community of outcasts, whose only common quality is anonymity, he stood out.

But Packo did not stand out for any reason you could see. His clothing and grooming were ragged as you would expect. Nothing in his appearance would make you believe he was different from any other homeless person. It was only if you spoke to him you discovered he was shockingly lucid even highly intelligent. He was well read and conversant in many topics. He displayed evidence of his education frequently sharing it with anyone who would take time to listen. He was knowledgeable about politics and current events, spending many hours poring over copies of newspapers in the public library. This kept his mind sharp and also provided shelter during inclement weather. He possessed knowledge of books and legends he had read in school. Among his boyhood favorites were *Moby Dick*, *Don Quixote* and other tales of high adventure or great endeavor. The legend of the lost city of Eldorado with its fabled golden treasure had especially captivated his childhood imagination. He would fanaticize that someday he would embark on a great quest like other famous heroes of literature or history.

His case workers were baffled over his strange life style. It was as if he chose to remain on the streets. But how could that be? He certainly seemed capable of holding a job. At first they would try to place him in local businesses and sometimes he would even accept menial jobs; dishwasher, busboy and the like. But over time they never seemed to work out and case workers eventually gave up. Some people just didn't want to be helped they assumed. Now he was nearing 60 and unlikely to change.

But no one knew the full story of how he came to live on the street. They could not know, because he never spoke of it. A disabled veteran, on his path to salvation, had chosen for no apparent reason to inhabit his personal purgatory. Neither did he reveal the promise he had made to remain there.

Packo had been given his nickname in Vietnam many years before. He was known to be a soft touch and willing to share his "Packo" smokes, or "Packo" gum. He had joined the Army right after graduation from Cass Tech High School. Patriotic and idealistic, he wanted to fight in his country's defense. He considered it a great honor to don the uniform and he vowed never to dishonor it. He arrived in-country in December 1967. He was assigned to C Company, 1st Battalion, 20th Infantry Regiment, 11th Brigade, of the 23rd American Infantry Division. His platoon commander was 2 LT William Calley under company commander CPT Earnest Medina. The first three months saw no direct contact with the enemy but the unit still suffered 28 casualties from mines and booby traps.

As part of a mop of the Tet Offensive, Packo's unit was assigned a search and destroy mission in a small group of hamlets collectively called My Lai. The mission was to locate and engage any pockets of Viet Cong remaining in the area. On the evening of March 15, Medina met with his platoon commanders to issue operational orders. When asked how to treat civilian non-com populations in the villages; Medina replied, "They're all VC now go out and get them". He believed all civilian non-coms would be absent at the time of the attack. Anyone remaining was presumed to be enemy Viet Cong. He ordered them to destroy anything "walking, crawling, or growing". His orders had come down from higher up. His brigade commander had directed them to "go in there aggressively, close with the enemy and wipe them out for good". Similar orders were issued to burn the houses, destroy food supplies, and kill the livestock.

What happened the next day was a murderous rampage. Somewhere between 300-500 (the official counts vary) Vietnamese men, women, and children were gunned down by American soldiers in a display of brutality seldom equaled in all the long bloody history of warfare. A few women had been attacked and assaulted before being shot. Packo was utterly horrified by what he saw. The worst moment occurred when he saw a young girl being chased by a soldier with a wild crazed look in his eye. He tried to reach out to the terrified child but he was too slow. The soldier was upon her before he could lift a finger. When it was over he sobbed uncontrollably until he vomited violently. He had not participated in the murderous madness, had not even fired his gun. But he was tormented by the feeling he should have done something to stop it.

The world was shocked and horrified by these events. Support for the war effort plummeted at home. In March 1968; President Johnson bowed out for the upcoming election in part because of the hideous butchery in Vietnam. Soldiers returning home, under a cloud of collective guilt, were treated with hostility by their countrymen. Packo left the Army in 1969 and returned to Detroit. He moved into his parents' home and tried to pick up the pieces but he was never the same after his homecoming. His parents were supportive but they knew when Louis retreated into depression, they could do little to help. Frequently nightmares tormented him and he sometimes sank into alcohol abuse. With time and patience his parents were able to pull him back from the brink. Gradually, he seemed to turn the corner towards sobriety. He had always been skilled with machinery so he was able to land a good job as a mechanic. He saved nearly everything he earned and prospered modestly as the years passed. In time he bought a small house and moved away from his parents' home. By the Bicentennial year of 1976, both his parents had passed away. He saw to their funeral and internment expenses at Woodlawn Cometery just west of Woodward Avenue. Planning ahead, he prearranged his own funeral expenses to occupy a plot in the same cemetery. When that time came, he could not depend on anyone to fill his final wishes. Nothing fancy, just a small stone. There were no available plots near his parents but there was always donated space where indigents were buried. That was good enough for him.

He lived in quiet anonymity through the next three decades. But the horrifying events of September 11, 2001, and the outbreak of war in Iraq and Afghanistan soon after; triggered a relapse and he started drinking heavily again. By early 2002, in his 52nd year, he hit rock bottom. When his house was destroyed by arson on the eve of Halloween, the notorious night of lawlessness and pillage known in Detroit as Devil's Night; he joined the pitiful ranks of Detroit's homeless. He still had an account in the bank but he seldom withdrew any money from it. On occasion, when a homeless acquaintance was especially desperate, he would gift them with a small amount of money to help them survive. But he was very careful with this generosity knowing he would be victimized by other homeless people if they knew he had money. So the years went by living in poverty on the street while possessing the financial means to end his suffering. In Packo's mind, this served as his personal penance for his days in Vietnam.

In 2003 Packo first met Arturo "Big A" Molina, a homeless Vietnam vet like himself. A big man, six and a half feet tall, he was generally avoided by other street people, perceived as a threat. He has been on the street for 18 months. His health was not good and his mental state was very erratic. He had suffered the loss of three toes due to frostbite which greatly hobbled him. But despite all that he managed to stay alive. He met Packo for the first time at the library one autumn afternoon, trying to steal a bit of warmth. Neither perceived a threat from the other, so they became occasional companions, never close friends. On the streets you had no friends. Sometimes they would pass a bottle between them exchanging few words, silently sharing their misery. Big A's health continued to fail. He lapsed into paranoid delusion more frequently. Packo sensed the end of the line was drawing near for the big man and doubted he would survive the oncoming winter. In early 2004, Big A passed away on a cold night on a deserted street off Mack Avenue in Detroit. Packo was with him at the end. The big man had insisted on going to this neighborhood, even though it was far from their normal haunts. He had prevailed on Packo to accompany him. Big A's mind was clear and he stared at Packo through bleary eyes. In a quiet raspy voice he shared the secret of his treasure, a tale he had never told anyone. The story he told would launch a quest that would occupy Packo for the rest of his life.

"When I gets back from 'Nam, I'se hurting real bad. No work and broke. Had to make money." He sucked in his breath painfully before continuing. "I steals it anywhere I can. Kills sometimes. Got to be big, lotsa money, maybe 30 grand. I'se scared someone kill me and take the money. So I hides it. I break in the old train station and puts in a secret place. 10th floor, you find it tween the stair and bathroom. In the flo'. Hid real good. You find that money. You give to my little girl. She grown now; Got picture…"

When Big A finished these words he abruptly collapsed on the street and breathed his last. He held in his lifeless hand a scrap of newspaper. Packo examined it carefully. It was torn from a month old copy of the Detroit Free Press. It was a profile along with a photo of a new social worker at a Salvation Army outpost nearby.

Big A never told him he had a daughter. Wonder if he even knew? Wonder if this fragment of newsprint informed him? Packo slid the scrap into his coat pocket. He gently closed the eyes of the corpse. "Rest easy, big man. You be free now. I'll take care of everything."

The next day Packo stood in front of the hulking wreck of the train station. He had seen it hundreds of times, even entered it once. But today he saw it differently, as if for the first time. Within those mysterious walls a great treasure lay hidden. On the 10th floor was Eldorado.

Packo began his great quest that very day. Entering the building was neither safe not easy. The police put up fences arround the perimeter of the property. If you could get by the fence, you could get close to the building. If you go that far, you had to avoid detection by police and private security surveillance. If you timed it right and were lucky you just might make it in. All the windows were broken out and the doors had been jimmied so there was no shortage of ways to enter. Once inside, many dangers remained: unsafe floors and stairways, falling debris, wild animals, and potentially most dangerous of all, other humans. Homeless people, thrill seekers, and drug dealers all infrequently invaded the space. These marauders would loot the property for anything of value or souvenirs. It was also a likely place to stash any contraband needing a safe hiding place.

Packo grew adept at getting by the fence and security. He did not make it in every time he tried but he got in often enough. Packo did not reach the 10th floor on the first try, nor on the 2nd try, nor the third. Each time he found the way blocked by some impassable barrier. But finally after six months of failed efforts, he found a clear passage and reached the 10th floor. He searched all day till the darkness in the hallway made it impossible to search and too dangerous to leave. So he spent a miserable night huddled in a corner waiting for dawn to continue the search. He searched the 10th floor time and again during that first year. He suspected that Big A made a mistake about the floor where he had hidden the treasure. So where to search next?

For the next five years he wandered the dark halls of the abandoned station floor by floor, whenever he could get in the building. He experienced many grave dangers and faced death several times. Once he surprised a hungry coyote wandering the halls and just managed to escape, the beast nipping at his heels. Another time he observed a drug dealer concluding a buy with some dangerous looking men. Something seemed to go wrong and everyone reached for their coat pockets. Packo managed to get away unseen before the sound of gunfire echoed from inside.

Now Packo himself sensed he was nearing the end of the line. He was nearing 60 and years of living on the street and his relentless search had taken its toll. He walked slowly, supporting himself with a cane. Five years of searching had come to nothing. Now he openly doubted Big A had hidden anything in these empty halls. If he had, someone else had found the treasure long ago. Packo would never know. But always he would look at the faded scrap of newspaper. A daughter deserved her father's legacy he would think to himself. And he would keep trying. But a day came when he knew the quest was over. He had a premonition, almost as if the building were beckoning him that he should try one last time. Before he entered the building that evening, he composed a letter to the woman whose faded photo he had carried for five years. He placed his letter in an envelope along with the scrap of newsprint. He posted the letter to an address on Mack Avenue that had been printed beneath her photo. It was a short message:

Dear Sybil

I knew your father. He was a good man. He had bad luck and lived a hard life. I was with him when he died. He loved you very much. His last words were about you. He had some money he wanted to give you but I can't find it. I did my best.

When he entered the building he immediately knew something was going on in the darkness ahead. He heard voices, one of them a woman's. He could tell there was a struggle underway. He cautiously approached the sound. He turned a corner and saw a man standing over a cowering young girl, bound by the wrists and whimpering pitifully. Packo froze for a moment. In his mind he flashed back to a bloody morning forty years before when he watched another helpless girl terrorized by a thug. Without hesitation he attacked the man swinging his cane wildly. His military training from so long ago was suddenly remembered. He was old now and slow but his blows were well placed. Soon the assailant lay sprawled on the floor, blood spurting from his mouth, spitting broken teeth, Packo hurriedly picked up the girl in his arms and staggered, as fast as he was able, for the way out. She had been beaten and was quite limp. She needed a doctor quickly. He sensed movement behind him, heard the muffled noise of an angry voice followed by the loud bang of a gunshot. Instantly he felt searing pain in his back. "Can't stop now. Can't stop now. Just a little farther…"

Packo somehow made it to the street just as passing police car was cruising by. He stepped in the path of the oncoming vehicle and it skidded to a stop an instant before running them over. "Please" Packo screamed. "She needs a doctor". He delivered the girl to the arms of one of the police officers, staggered for a moment then collapsed in the street. The other officer hunched over Packo giving him a perfunctory examination. He checked the limp body for a pulse or breath noises. "Never mind this one, he's gone." Looking at his shabby clothes and grooming he said with barely concealed contempt. "Why do they live like this?"

Many soldiers came home from Vietnam in a body bag, others with lost limbs or sanity. A few, like Packo, came home with serious wounds to their very soul. These last were the hardest to heal. They wore no battle scars that could be seen, but the damage was as traumatic as any inflicted by bomb or bullet. For these tragic figures, the war dragged on, never ending. Packo had searched years for his illusory treasure through the dark, dangerous wreckage of his conscience and Michigan Central Station. In the end he found only valor and reconciliation. His war was over at last. Packo had found Eldorado.

Whistle Stop 26

JANUARY 14, 2010

The Search

Sybil Molina reread the tear stained page for the third time. A fresh set of tears feel onto the paper. She had received a letter this morning at her office in the Salvation Army mission where she was employed as a social worker. She was completely perplexed by the brief note and a faded clipping of newsprint contained in the smudged, creased envelope. The letter was recently and locally postmarked and was addressed by a spidery hard to read cursive. Her father Artie had been killed many years ago in Vietnam. Yet here was an anonymous letter from someone claiming to have known her father and to have been with him when he died.

Equally confusing, was the clipping from a five year old copy of the Free Press published the week of her arrival in this office. This was obviously a case of mistaken identity. What else could it be? For a moment the thought occurred to her the letter may have come from an old army buddy he had served with in Vietnam who had been present when her father died. But why would the letter writer wait forty years to contact her? The letter bore no return address to enable a trace. The appearance of the letter suggested the author was an elderly, possibly homeless person. As a case worker, she worked frequently with the destitute; trying to find them jobs and see to their basic needs; but that explained nothing. Her mother had died only recently so could not help solve the mystery. She was still puzzling over this momentous news when she left for home that afternoon.

She had lived with her mother Beth for several years. The two had shared a flat nearby and Sybil had cared for her mother in her failing health. Beth spoke frequently of her husband Artie. She would return in her mind to a happier time when Artie was home and Sybil was a little girl. Beth was proud to display, the Purple Heart and Silver Star Artie had been awarded for his heroism in combat. Sybil had been very young when her Dad left and her memories had faded over the years. All she could remember was that he was a very large man. She struggled to find his image in her deepest memories but it was vague and uncertain. She resolved to try and solve the mystery but she really did not know where to start. Could her father have survived Vietnam? If that were true she wanted to find his grave.

The letter Sybil received left out crucial information which would have directed her search. For starters, Big A had died five years before Packo had written his letter. If she began the search looking at recent deaths she would be fruitlessly searching the wrong years. Neither did the letter make any reference to a place. The envelope had been postmarked in Detroit only a week before so it suggested the deceased had died locally. But where? It was a big city with many unidentified, unclaimed dead. Lastly, the letter gave no description or identifying information that could circumstantially point to Arturo Molina. It could have been some other unfortunate and this letter sent to her by mistake. Sybil first had to decide whether she was willing to believe this could be her dad. If she felt there was a chance it MIGHT be him, then she would search for him. For the moment, the complexity of the problem overwhelmed her. She had always accepted her father had died in Vietnam. Unless she had more to go on she reluctantly chose to continue to believe that. Still enough doubt lingered that she kept the letter.

Later that afternoon, Sybil, went into her mother's bedroom. She had mostly stayed out of it since Beth died except to clean. She had found it too painful to sort through her letters and keepsakes. Today she was drawn to the bureau drawer where she knew Arties medals were kept. She removed the box and carefully opened the cover. To her surprise, there were several documents inside she had never seen before. The first was an official looking telegram, the second a handwritten letter. The third document was single sheet of notebook paper with a handwritten name, address, and phone number in neat cursive. The name "George Holloway" on the sheet was unknown to her. She recognized the address from a city block that had been torn down years before when the freeway was widened. She picked up her phone and called the number and learned it was no longer in service. She next turned her attention to the telegram dated 1967. It was sent from a VA hospital in New Jersey, reporting that Arturo Molina had been honorably discharged from the army. She next unfolded the letter. It was from her father, Artie. Tears clouded her eyes as she read the words.

Dearest Beth   May 18th, 1967

By now you know I am out of the Army. I was in the hospital here for three months after leaving Vietnam. Doctors say I am getting better but I am afraid to come home now. I am so jittery and angry all the time that I sometimes just explode. I almost slugged a nurse the other day because she came up behind and spooked me. I get nightmares real bad and my nerves are always on edge. I hope to get better but I am afraid of what I might do to you or Sybil. I will try and send money when I can. But it is best if you just forget me. I am so very sorry. Kiss Sybil for me.

Love, Artie

The heartbreaking letter confirmed what Sybil had chosen not to believe. Artie had not died in Vietnam, so the person described in the letter could well have been him. Applying her deduction that the author of the letter was probably an elderly, homeless, local person, she at least had a place to start. She would begin by searching all the recent deaths of indigent men in Detroit. No small task.

Arturo Molina was immediately called Big A when he arrived in Vietnam. His impressive size and strength made him a little scary to all the other boots in his outfit. He pulled his share of dangerous duty and had survived several firefights. He seemed to come through the fighting unharmed but inside his head, the tension of walking patrol through the bush, on a search and destroy mission, really got to him. The battle, in which he earned his medals, was horrible. Bodies everywhere. Explosions all around. He had been terrified. He took a round in the shoulder which shattered his collar bone but he still managed to take out an enemy machine gun with a hand grenade. It was the first time he had knowingly killed men and it troubled him greatly. In the midst of all the gore and chaos, at the peak of the battle, he was able to save two other soldiers in his patrol, including his commanding officer, 2nd Lieutenant Jackson Holloway a fellow Detroiter. Both the lieutenant and Molina suffered serious injuries that required evacuation to military hospitals in Germany and the US.

When Artie shipped out stateside, he submitted himself to a VA hospital in New Jersey. His nightmares tormented him. He would awaken drenched in sweat and heart pounding, horrified by hallucinations of bodies being blown to bits, and him bathed in blood. Post-Traumatic Stress Disorder was a known disorder among retuning GI's; but drug therapy and counseling could not seem to help Artie. His doctors eventually concluded he could get better care outside the military and discharged him. But Big A knew he was too dangerous to return to his family. He had a hair trigger temper, ready to explode at any provocation or loud noise. Artie wrote his farewell letter to his family and went on the road. His decades long wandering carried him all across the country trying to find peace of mind. His decline into debilitating mental illness was gradual. He had periods of lucidity during which he worked and even sent money home to Beth and Sybil. But inside the bomb kept ticking. During his darker moods he would self-medicate with alcohol, and his downward spiral accelerated. His paranoid delusions would abate temporarily, but inevitably return.

It was during these days of wandering that Big A started accumulating the treasure that would one day drive Packo on his quest. When he arrived in a new town he would usually find quick employment as a bouncer in rough bars and after hours joints. His intimidating presence and nasty disposition were the only resume his employers required. In time, his talents would land him a gig as a body guard for some famous or notorious client who needed his muscle. But inevitably, his violent temper would get the best of him and he would have to skip town ahead of the police after beating some unfortunate man senseless in a fight. Most of his employers concluded he was just too dangerous to keep on the payroll. His longest sojourn on his lengthy odyssey was the 7 years he lived in Nashville, Tennessee. There the climate was agreeably mild compared to Detroit and there was no shortage of honkytonk bars and music celebrities to employ him. He also spent 6 years in Dallas where he found plentiful work in the many clubs of Deep Ellum. While living in Dallas he took up with a cocktail waitress and the two lived in a rented home not far from the Texas State fair ground. That affair ended when he beat a man to death in a dispute over money. So it was a quick escape and back on the road. The years slipped by quickly. Over the course of the next 20 years his health declined, from encroaching age and the damage inflicted by so many years of violent living. His store of cash would rise and fall depending on his luck, as he wandered around the country. When he was on the move, he carried the cash in a canvas duffle bag that never left his sight. By the time his treasure was moved inside the ruins of Michigan Central Station it amounted to over $25,000-the most money he had seen since leaving the army. But always in the back of his mind was the yearning to return to his family. He desperately desired to present his treasure to his wife and daughter to help fill the hole of regret in his heart.

In time he was drawn irresistibly to return to Detroit. Until he could find a way to reunite with his family he would bide his time on the streets. He was not certain he knew the current address of his wife and daughter since he had been gone so many years. When he had sent money home during his absence, it was addressed to a PO Box, so that did not help him. He went to the church he knew Beth had attended at the time he had left town. The minister there delivered to him the terrible news that Beth had died only a month before. It was as if a bright light had gone out. Consumed by guilt and regret, he could not bring himself to contact his now adult daughter, Sybil. He was still fearful about abruptly reentering her life. He determined he would do everything he could to get clean and sober. Only then would he reconcile with his little girl and deliver to her his treasure. The ruins of the train station were reasonably secure from the elements so he took up residence there. His treasure was not so much hidden there as it was misplaced. Big A had carelessly left his stash unattended in the deserted main waiting room while he wandered an adjacent hallway in a drunken stupor. He may have passed out or fallen asleep but when he returned, it was gone. Big A searched for it, in vain. He wandered the hallways all the way to the 9th floor, but could never make it higher because the way was blocked. In his addled mind he became convinced he had hidden his treasure on the tenth floor. It was safe, he reassured himself, for the time being, until he could find a way to retrieve it.

Sybil soon found out what an impossible task she had given herself. She called hospitals, social services, newspaper, police offices, and churches searching for clues. The only thing she had to go on was the person she sought was a deceased, very tall black man in his late 60's or early 70's. She did not know if it was a homicide or natural causes. She assumed that a homicide would be recorded by the police department, and possibly by the newspaper or TV journalists, but a death of natural cause might be unnoticed. She learned to her great sadness, that the previous winter many homeless people froze to death. Most were never claimed nor identified. Anonymous in life, forgotten in death.

Sybil resigned herself to the likelihood she would never find her father's grave. She resolved to get on with her work. She would continue to hope but the task just was not possible without some more information. But months passed with no new leads.

Social Services had referred a new case to Sybil. A young woman aged 17 named Clarisse Jackson would be assigned to her case load. Sybil studied her file. For one so young it chronicled a long depressing list of misfortune. Orphaned young, abused as a child, school dropout, in and out of foster homes, sometimes homeless, vagrant. Sybil sighed as she read the list. One event on the report caught her eye. The previous November she had been abducted and held captive in the ruins of Michigan Central Station. She had been rescued by a homeless man who managed to free her but was gunned down in the process. The police report had included interviews of several persons who knew the man. Sybil vaguely remembered the incident from the newspapers.

On an impulse she picked up the telephone and called her friend Charley Watters at the *Free Press*. He had worked the city beat for years and knew as much about the homeless community as anyone, having been homeless himself as a youngster. Charley had managed to escape his life on the streets, get an education and eventually land a job as a reporter. He brought instincts and sensitivity to his reporting and Sybil had worked with him in the past. Sybil had consulted him early during her search for her father but he had little to go on and could not provide much help. This time it was different. The gunshot victim who had rescued Clarisse was a known person who could be investigated. If he had left any tracks at all with Social Services he might be found. Charley said he would get back to her.

Sybil did what she could for Clarisse. She interviewed her about her personal history and helped her enroll in a high school GED program. She gave her suggestions on employment opportunities and provided the names of pastors to help her. She outlined the range of social services she was eligible to receive. She eventually asked Clarisse about her harrowing escape in the ruins of the railroad station. Clarisse could not remember much. She vaguely remembered her attacker, blacking out, and coming to in the hospital. She had no memory of her rescuer.

It was the next day when Charley called Sybil back. The dossier he had acquired from the police reports was thin but quite revealing. The man had been identified as Louis Ochoa a 60 year old Vietnam veteran. Went by the name Packo. No known address, No known relatives, believed to be homeless since at least 2002. High School graduate, previously owned a home destroyed by arson, frequently observed in the vicinity of the abandoned railroad station. Was known to give money to other homeless persons; paid funeral and burial expenses for another homeless man in 2004.

This last bit of knowledge immediately caught her attention. She wondered if the homeless man whose burial expenses Ochoa had paid had some connection to her dad. She had to find out more about that unfortunate man. Sybil asked Charley to try and find out any information on the deceased.

Charley contacted the funeral home where Artie's body had been sent five years ago. The records were incomplete but still on file. An elderly unidentified black man, late 60's or early 70's, very tall; only name on record "Big A", interred at Woodlawn Cemetery in a donated burial plot. The scant information in his obituary indicated he was a Vietnam veteran who had battled PTSD after leaving the Army.

Sybil gasped. The web of circumstantial evidence seemed to be tightening around these two deceased homeless men. After all, if Ochoa had cared enough to go through the effort and expense to bury her father, a personal letter to his daughter would certainly be appropriate. The pieces began to fall together. The letter was not written at the time of Artie's death but 5 years later. Why the delay? Why had Ochoa waited so long to send it? Maybe the reference to looking for lost money was the key to the mystery. Was that the answer? Her most convincing evidence was the name "Big A" on the funeral home paperwork consistent with a very tall man named Arturo. Her last doubts were crumbling so she resolved to go see the grave for herself. On the following Saturday she rode the bus to the historic burial grounds. So much history. so many illustrious Detroiters resting here, among whose number she hoped to find a person lost to history. The donated burial plots were untidy and covered with a sparse growth of weeds. She strolled among them until she spotted a small marker flush with the ground, Packo's final gift. A small unadorned stone with the simple inscription: "Big A". Sybil knew that she had found the only monument to the life and struggles of this unhappy man; the only evidence of his existence in this world. She produced from her handbag a small American flag and inserted it into the ground next to the stone. The flag snapped to attention in the gentle breeze.

Her meditation continued for several minutes, trying to roll back the years to her childhood, hoping to catch once more a glimpse of the face of the man she called Papa. Finally her thoughts were interrupted by a sidelong glance at the grave marker next to her father's. A similar stone, so alike in composition and dimension, they may have been cut from a single block; inscribed simply "Louis Ochoa". The name was familiar but she could not instantly place it. Then a smile of recognition and wonderment crossed her face. Here at last the benefactor of her luckless father had found his resting place. It seemed fitting that these comrades in war and companions in misfortune should lie side by side. Both had battled demons beyond Sybil's understanding but here in this quiet and neglected space had finally found peace. The faint echoes of Vietnam were subsiding into silence. The ripples that extended in widening circles for so long from that terrible war were settling into the glassy stillness of reconciliation.

Whistle Stop 27

JULY 20, 2018

The Return

The ruins of Michigan Central continued to brood over the city during the station's centennial year 2013. This momentous anniversary was neither celebrated nor noticed by most Detroiters. The station's long dormancy became symbolic of municipal indecision and mismanagement. It remained a sullen presence, an upsetting hulk, abiding its long hibernation. It disfigured the city skyline as a jagged broken tooth defaces a genial smile. Visitors to the city, as well as downtown residents would scratch their heads and wonder aloud why it had not been torn down long ago. For three decades it had stood empty and unused. Its vacancy was a feral threat to the community as it harbored, God knows what, types of lawlessness and danger. Through the years numerous proposals had been made to repurpose the structure, but none of them panned out. In the meantime the sad old building continued its long slow decay.

This depressing condition of the station was all that Clarisse Jackson ever knew. It was a forlorn fixture presiding over every day of her childhood. She had played in neighborhood streets in the very shadow of the abandoned building. She had even, as a youngster, entered the building on a dare. She found it dirty and scary. On another occasion, nine years before, she had been forced into the building against her will, abducted and terrorized by a brutal stranger. She would still shudder when she thought of that awful night. Now when she passed the building, she would quicken her pace. She also had a faint memory, or possibly just awareness from being told so frequently, that a homeless man had been her savior that night.

Clarisse had put that all that behind her. Shortly after she was released from the hospital following her rescue she was assigned to the caseload of a social worker named Sybil Molina. Sybil had turned out to be a second savior to the young girl. Based on Sybil's advice and tutoring Clarisse had earned her high school equivalency. She had found a job in a downtown McDonald's restaurant and had proved to be a dependable worker. Each step forward was followed by another step. There were setbacks along the way but these were overcome. Clarisse was forced from her foster residence, and Sybil had taken her in until she could land on her feet. As the years went by, that arrangement had become permanent. Sybil was like an older sister to Clarisse. With Sybil's help, Clarisse had completed junior college and went on to attend Wayne State University. Now she pondered what she wanted to do with her life. She, like many who came from hardscrabble circumstances, aspired to a career where she could return some good to the world. Above all else, she was passionately committed to social and economic justice. She wanted to help the poor.

Clarisse, with the help and encouragement of Charley Watters, old friend and mentor of Sybil's, decided to pursue a career in journalism.

She concluded that was the best way for her to serve as advocate for social justice. Charley had arranged introductions, leading to interviews, which secured her an entry level position at the NBC affiliate in Detroit. She was attractive, well spoken, and confident. Her bosses at the TV station were impressed by her determination and work ethic in overcoming enormous odds. Her "Q" scores, the industry standard of evaluating favorability of on air personalities, had been strong. Moreover, she was a home grown personality and a powerful human interest story. All in all she seemed to personify the virtues that Detroiters like to think describe their city; perseverance against long odds and overcoming obstacles. She was what they called in the business a "natural". Added to that, she had the great good fortune of being in the right place at the right time. It was not long before she was doing remote shoots at community events, art fairs, concerts, festivals and the like. It was assumed with luck and experience she might become a local newscaster someday. Clarisse had come so far in such a short time she could scarcely believe it herself.

In time she met a young man, Hector Gonzales, who after honorable military service in Iraq had enrolled in Law School at the University of Michigan and was now in his second year. He, like Clarisse, had risen from adversity in his youth on the strength of hard work and determination. In time, the two young people fell in love. The future looked bright for the young couple. Clarisse shared with Hector how her life had been saved by a homeless stranger and the generosity of a local social worker. Hector had a similar story. They discovered their mutual connection to the ruins of Michigan Central that had bent their fates toward each other. It was, as if, destiny had taken a hand in bringing them together. No one was more gratified by Clarisse's progress than Sybil Molina, knowing that she was instrumental to her friend's remarkable turnaround.

Sybil and Clarisse continued to make regular visits to Woodlawn Cemetery to visit the graves of Artie and Packo. Neither of the women had personally known these men. But both women felt a deep and sincere connection. Over time they began to relate to the deceased in a personal way, such as: "I wonder what Dad would want me to do"; or "I wonder what Louis would say about this?" The living have always consulted the wisdom of their ancestors, secure in the belief that they were always listening. But Sybil had one unattended detail she wished to see accomplished before she died. She wanted to visit the Vietnam Memorial Wall in Washington D.C. She knew her Dad had not died in Vietnam, nor did she think some clerical error might have inscribed his name on the wall. But Sybil wanted to make a final gesture of respect in honor of all those who survived but later succumbed to mental disability. She had seen on television and read in printed media how surviving family would place personal memorials before the wall. She had learned all the letters, mementos and testimonials were carefully collected and preserved by the Parks department. She wanted to tell the story of Artie and Packo so that in some small way their memory would survive.

She began to write their story. There were many blanks she would never be able to fill in. She knew nothing about Eldorado, or the quest that Packo had promised Artie on her behalf. But what she did know and recorded was an emotional tribute to the two men. It concluded with a heartfelt plea that such as these must not be forgotten, either alive or after death. Their names did not appear on the wall but they were no less victims of that war. Finally satisfied with her story she placed it in an envelope along with copies of the letter Packo had written her, Artie's farewell letter to Beth, and the faded scrap of newsprint with her photo that Artie and Packo had carried for so many years. The originals of these, too personal to relinquish, remained with Arties medals in a bureau drawer in her home.

Sybil and Clarisse arrived in Washington on a cold gray day in early spring. They both spent a long time standing in contemplation before the black granite wall. So many names, so many stories to tell of lost loved ones and crushed ambitions. Clarisse, being younger, had no direct connection with the war, nor any memories of it. She tried to visualize Packo as a young man. She wished she could have known him then. She wondered if his hopes for the future were as bright as hers were now. Sybil, inclined her head, and rested her forehead on the cool stone. She whispered a simple "I love you Daddy". She then placed the envelope on the ground resting against the base of the wall. All up and down the length of the wall they observed many such offerings. Teddy bears, bundles of flowers, military badges and insignia, and many envelopes resembling hers. After some moments of quite reflection, they withdrew.

In June of 2018, came the momentous news that the Ford Motor Company had purchased the old Michigan Central Building intending to restore it and convert it for use as a futuristic Tech Center. The symbolism of Ford returning to its roots in the city was praised by civic leaders. For the first time in decades the old building created a stir of interest and energy. It was widely predicted the city would experience a great renewal. Ford executives offered the public a chance to enter the station for a view before the renovation began. The response was overwhelming. Though pre-registration was required for entry, far more interested persons showed up than could be admitted. People waited in long lines for hours in steamy humidity hoping for a chance to get in. Many were turned away disappointed. The local news stations were all there to cover the event. Among these was Clarisse Jackson Channel 4 news, interviewing those in the queue.

She had been hesitant about the assignment at first. Her memories of the station were terrifying and she did not like remembering that time in her life. She knew she would be expected to enter the building. The thought scared her a little. She briefly considered turning down the assignment, but in the end, she concluded that it was the right thing to confront her past. She decided that history had no power, except to teach. She wrote a brief script for her on air report. The TV audience that saw and heard her narration had little idea of her personal catharsis as she spoke. The message was simple, but spoken from a wellspring of emotion. All that had happened to her, and all that she hoped to be; were blended in her life story. The great building reflected that fusion as well.

"The old railroad station has loomed over this Detroit neighborhood, in good times and bad for over a century. In its long history, we remember happy moments of heroism and prosperity. We also recall times of shame and regret. Everyone who ever used this station has a personal tale, a unique memory, to tell of the experience. Regardless of how we remember it, the past is the foundation upon which we build our future. Today begins a new chapter in a very long story. Just imagine all the tales left to be told by new generations of Detroiters. It is with them in mind, we take this first step toward a brighter future."

"Clarisse Jackson Channel 4 news reporting from outside Michigan Central Station."

Sybil was watching her friend on television. Her eyes welled when she heard her words. She thought of the mysterious intervention of fate that had merged her life story with Clarisse, Artie, and Packo. She thought of her envelope resting at the base of the Vietnam Memorial Wall. She knew that like the Michigan Central Station itself, the stories she had placed there would survive; the past reaching through the present to occupy its rightful place of honor in the future.

Whistle Stop 28

MARCH 30, 2003

The Gift

Hector Gonzales sucked in his breath and tried to blend into the dark hulking backdrop of Michigan Central Station. His back pressed the cold stone wall as he flattened himself trying to become invisible to anyone trying to find him. His eyes tried vainly to pierce the blackness to see if he was still being pursued by those who had chased him to the very doorway of the abandoned station. He carried a flashlight in his pocket with new batteries but he dared not to use it, fearing exposure. How did all this come about? It all happened so fast that Hector had no time to process his next step. He and his cousin Carlos Ruiz, and classmate

Jermain James, had been out on a harmless nighttime adventure drinking beer and doing a little urban exploring in the neighborhood alleys adjacent to the old railroad station. They had all heard rumors of the souvenirs one could sometimes find in the ruins of the old station. A friend who invaded the space had found and looted what was left of the cigar store, carrying out some old advertising signs and a highly prized wall clock. They had started the evening intending to try their luck with a treasure hunt of their own. The closer they got to the fence surrounding the property, the less appealing the adventure seemed. The building was not an inviting place by day, but by night it was dark and terrifying. They had just about talked themselves out of the attempt when they were confronted by five members of the Seven Mile Bloods, a Detroit street gang who were none too welcoming of these uninvited guests. The Bloods were feared for their fierce violence in defense of their turf, but surprisingly this neighborhood was not their usual territory. None of that mattered to the three friends. Whatever their reason for being there the danger was real and the threat to their lives was immediate. In the tense moment before weapons were drawn, the three friends broke and ran in separate directions. Hector had jumped the fence and headed for the abandoned station. He heard shouts and pounding footsteps followed by gunshots, but he could not see anything in the darkness. He heard shouts and footsteps approaching him. He held his breath until his lungs burned. Then in the awful moment before he was sure to be discovered, he saw a welcome but terrifying sight. The red light and sirens of police cars were speeding rapidly towards his position. Not knowing what else to do, Hector slipped quickly through a broken out window and carefully made his way down the long dark hallway inside. From the outside he could hear commotion as the police were searching the grounds. For the moment, Hector felt he was safe. Then the sound of the police appeared to grow louder as they seemed to be searching inside the station. The sound of their pursuit drove Hector farther along the hallway and deeper into the station. Eventually the scuffling noises of the searchers subsided as they abandoned their pursuit and all was deathly quiet. For the first time Hector reached into his pocket and drew out his flashlight. His original feeling of relief was quickly re-placed by a growing sense of dread as he realized his danger was not over. The beam of his flashlight allowed him to sees ahead into the gloom but did not reveal any way out. Now Hector was truly terrified of the oppressive darkness and the unknown threats around each corner. He was desperate to find the nearest exit. Facing the police or the scattered members of the gang could not be as fearful as this place. With an effort, he forced himself to be calm. He did his best to reassess his predicament. The most obvious escape was to retrace his steps and try to locate the broken window he originally entered. This seemed easy enough to do. But in the pitch blackness of the building he found it impossible to get his bearings. Had he inadvertently turned a corridor into some parallel hallway? So despite his plan, Hector found himself drawn into the maze of intersecting passages that lead him into deep recesses of the building. At length his flashlight revealed that he was in a cavernous space with an impossibly high ceiling. He deduced at once that he was in the great waiting room of the old terminal. The slightly luminous arcs on the wall were obviously exterior windows. These were barely a shade lighter than the inky blackness within the terminal. From beyond those translucent openings, the faint glow of illumination from the street penetrated the opaque walls. At this first revelation of a way out, Hector's terror began to ease. For the first time he relaxed enough to inspect his surroundings. The great expanse was awe inspiring and created the sensation of drifting through outer space. Gradually, Hector's vision became adjusted to the darkness and he was able to make out features of his surroundings. He perceived a structure that appeared to be a long counter upon which some long forgotten products had once been displayed for sale. Upon this counter, he could make out the shape of what appeared to be a large box the size of a typewriter. He remembered his friend who had entered the building and walked out with tokens from the old cigar store. Maybe these were more artifacts which could be sold. He picked up the box and felt its heft. There was something inside. Before he was able to pry open the lid which seemed to be sealed with tape. he jerked his head upright.

He sensed, more than heard, the approach of footsteps from somewhere nearby in the darkness. He was not alone in this fearful place. He strained his senses to identify the threat that appeared to be staggering toward his location. Hector tucked the box under his arm and as swiftly as he dared in the darkness, moved towards the exterior windows. He soon reached a wall and to his immense relief, found an unsealed door which screeched open to the outside on rusty hinges. Hector ran as fast as he could towards home.

When he arrived at home, he snuck past his father who was snoring loudly on the sofa facing the still playing TV set. He had fallen asleep waiting up for Hector's mother who worked the night shift as a nurse at St Mary's Hospital. Hector glanced at his watch, 11:30 PM. His mother would be home in under an hour. That gave Hector time to slip into his bedroom without waking his father. He used a scissors to cut the tape seal on the box. He was stunned by what he found inside. A large stash of cash filled the box nearly to the top. His hands shook as he inspected the numerous rolls of bills, all held in neat bundles bound by rubber bands. He closely inspected this treasure. It looked like loose currency not old, recently circulated. The denominations were mixed within each bundle. Some $100 bills all the way down to $5.00. He made a quick count and concluded there was well over $20,000 in the box. His lust over this treasure was short lived and gave way to instant panic. This money had to be dirty; almost certainly involving drugs or robbery. The persons who had stashed this treasure would surely be searching for it and would gladly kill to recover it. Hector knew he would not be safe until he could dispose of this money. He knew instinctively that anyone else who was aware of the money would also be under threat. Hector resolved not to share this information with anyone until he could figure out what to do. At the moment he was more concerned about staying alive than he was holding on to this money. The first order of business was to hide the money. In the backyard of his house was an old seldom used shed that had over the years housed rakes, shovels and other yard tools. He took all of the cash and placed it in a plastic trash bag. He then placed the bag inside a second heavy plastic contractor's disposal bag. These double bags he placed inside a plastic storage tub with a sealable lid. He was confident the money was safe from the elements. For fear of waking his father or encountering his mother he resolved to hide the money in the morning before school when his father would be at work and his mother asleep. In the meantime he hid the tub in his closet and fell into a fitful sleep.

The aftermath of that fateful evening persisted several months. His companions that night, Carlos and Jermaine, had both managed to escape. The gang members involved in the attempted shooting were apprehended, still Hector lived in terror that the rest of the gang would somehow discover the identity of the three strangers that had invaded their territory that night. Hector was certain that the money must have belonged to the Bloods and they had stashed it in the station for safe keeping. That would explain why the gang had just happened to be patrolling the perimeter of Michigan Central Station. But months passed, and no one confronted Hector and his companions. It seemed their identity had not been discovered by the gang. Just as importantly, the police never identified the three friends so they were not required to testify against the gang members. Lacking any evidence or witnesses the charges against the gang were reduced and the defendants were on the street in short order. So Hector's apprehension grew. This was a very dangerous moment, as Hector anticipated the released gang members would surely redouble their effort to find the intruders who had stolen their money.

Hector followed his plan and never breathed a word of what happened that night to anyone. He intended to share the money with his two friends if and when he felt it was safe. In the meantime the loot was hidden away where no one would find it. Just when Hector was starting to relax, his friend Jermaine was killed in a car crash. The police reported indicated a DUI was the cause, but Hector could not help wonder if the Bloods were involved and were catching up to them at last. Other murders had been covered up by similar "accidents". Jermaine was not known to be a hard drinker. Beyond that the car he was driving had been reported stolen and that all seemed suspicious. If Jermaine had run afoul of the gang, could he have given up the names of his two friends before he was killed?

At Jermaine's funeral, Carlos and Hector shared their fears. Neither of them had felt completely at ease since their confrontation with gang violence that night at Michigan Central. Carlos was the more fearful of the two and had the more desperate plan. Carlos announced his decision to enlist in the army, determined to flee gang retribution, and his abusive and domineering father as well. Hector reluctantly concluded Carlos was doing the right thing. Hector almost told him about the money held in trust for him. In the end, Hector concluded that holding on to the money a little longer was in his cousin's best interest. Carlos's father would surely take any money Carlos possessed. If Carlos got his share he would have to hide it anyway to keep it protected. It seemed the safest thing for Hector to keep his secret a little longer. He would split the cash when Carlos was sufficiently out of reach of his father and the gang.

After completing basic training Carlos had been stationed in Korea. Hector for his part resolved to go about his life as normally as possible and try not to attract any unwanted attention. He enrolled in the fall at Wayne State University. His family was not wealthy but did have adequate means to send him to college. Hector was a very good student and was able to earn scholarships along the way. He never considered spending the money for school expenses because in his mind, half of it belonged to his cousin. He would split it with him when he returned from the army.

Four years later, Hector graduated with high honors from Wayne State. Upon graduating he joined the Navy and was accepted to Navy Seal training. He was in very good physical condition and had the right blend of intelligence and discipline. He passed the rigorous training and eventually became part of the elite Seal Team Six that hunted down Osama Bin Laden and brought him to justice. Hector had performed his part of the mission skillfully and was awarded high commendations. Hector liked the military but only briefly considered making it his career. He had other ambitions. He decided to return home and attend law school. His parents were aging and he wanted to be near enough to care for them. Hector applied to, and was admitted to the University of Michigan School of Law.

Hector tried to keep in touch with Carlos but 5 years passed quickly with no word as to his whereabouts. Carlos' father was in prison and his mother had passed away so there was no one to supply Hector any information. Hector decided he would not break his trust. He was sure the two cousins would meet again someday. In the meantime, the money was safe. He had long since overcome his fear that people were still searching for it. He didn't need the money for his own personal expenses and his parents were doing well enough so he was in no hurry to tap the funds. It could remain safely in hiding indefinitely until he could discharge his debt.

It was in his second year at law school that Hector met Clarisse Jackson. He recognized her at once from one of her television appearances. She was doing research at the library where Hector studied. He was instantly attracted to the pretty young woman and after summoning his nerve approached her and asked her out for coffee. Their mutual attraction deepened over time and it soon was obvious they were made for each other. Both had overcome difficult starts in life and were now embarking on bright futures. The couple began to plan their lives together. In time they each shared their stories and discovered even greater similarities. Most surprising of all was their individual experiences in Michigan Central Station. Over the years neither had been eager to share their stories and for the most part kept those events secret. But they discovered they both had profound turning points that occurred in the old train station. Hector's story greatly impressed Clarisse. Hector had held this vast sum in trust for his cousin all these years. She concluded this reflected high moral character and she loved him all the more for it. She was not interested herself in acquiring the money since she was doing well and didn't really need it. She even suggested giving Hector's share away to some worthy charity to help others on their life's journeys.

The couple married in the fall of 2018. Sybil Molina served the ceremonial role of mother of the bride. Hector's father walked Clarisse down the aisle. The couple exchanged their vows in old St Anne's Church in Mexicantown since it was Hector's home parish growing up. It was a beautiful occasion with many of Hector's friends from the Navy and from law school in attendance. Clarisse as a local television celebrity had a large gathering of friends and well-wishers. The church was filled to capacity. After the ceremony Hector got the surprise of his life as he was processing out of the church with Clarisse on his arm. Sitting in the very last row of pews, close to the wall, Hector could swear he saw his cousin Carlos. He couldn't be sure because the man's appearance was nothing like Hector remembered. But the resemblance was striking. The man did not raise his gaze towards the couple. Instead his face was pointed downward as if trying to avoid eye contact. Hector wanted to investigate this unrecognized guest but was swept up in the rush of well-wishers and could not break away. By the time the crowd of his friends and families had disappeared he saw that the stranger had gone. For the moment, Hector, let the stranger slip from his mind. The wedding reception was to be held in a local restaurant on Bagley Street a short distance from the church. Just as dinner was finished and the party and dancing were revving up, Hector noticed against the wall, unmistakably this time, his cousin Carlos. He rushed forward to embrace him leaving Clarisse in a circle of her television colleagues.

Yes, it was Carlos but he was so different from the boy Hector had shared his life with growing up. Instead of the friendly open expression he now had a predatory look about him, his eyes darting back and forth over the scene, as if hunting. The collar of his shirt barely concealed the tattoos on his neck. He had metal studs piercing his nose and ears. Hector was still overjoyed to see him despite his shocking appearance. They retreated to a remote table at the edge of the dance floor. There Carlos told his story. The decision to join the Army had been a disaster. He was constantly getting into trouble in his unit and was in and out of the brig for a series of ever more serious charges including being AWOL for an extended time on a drunken binge. He next became involved with drug trafficking. He was dishonorably discharged for his bad conduct. He had returned to Detroit seven years ago. His military record against him, he was unable to find a job. He had fallen into a swirling vortex of gang violence and drug abuse. The most shocking part of his story was he now was a member of the Bloods, the very same gang that had terrorized the friends that night near Michigan Central Station so many years ago. Hector found the story tragic and he was filled with pity for his boyhood comrade. Disturbingly, Carlos did not seem to display any remorse or sense of responsibility for his bad behavior. Eventually he came to the point of his desired reunion with Hector. He had seen the wedding notice in the paper and decided he would crash the party. Always on the hustle, he thought he could coax some money out of Hector. He figured on his wedding day he was likely to have money or bridal gifts that could be turned into quick cash. It was the cold detached way he related this story that turned Hector's pity into disgust. He now knew the cousin he had shared so much with was no more. He got up from the table.

"I won't talk about this now; For God's sake this is my wedding day. But I will meet you tomorrow at 11:00 am at Clark Park near the swing set."

After he said this Hector turned and walked away broken hearted and angry for his cousin's disgraceful downfall.

The newlyweds were going on a quick honeymoon to Traverse City. Neither of them could afford to be gone for very long. They would go to Europe as soon as they could see clear. Clarisse had always wanted to see Paris. Hector told Clarisse he had some unfinished business to be attended to before they left town the next day. She should finish packing and he would be back after lunch.

His first stop that morning was to retrieve the money from the hiding place behind his father's home. It had remained there safely in hiding all these years. Hector recalled the terror of the night that this fortune had come to him. He thought of his two boyhood comrades who unknowingly had been intended shareholders to this windfall. He breathed a quiet prayer in Jermaine's memory and an equally fervent one for Carlos's rehabilitation. He removed a short stack of bills and placed the remaining currency into a large grocery bag. He next headed to Clark Park where he found Carlos waiting. Without preamble, Hector handed a small stack of bills to Carlos who after a quick count stuck it in his pocket. Hector said as he turned to walk away.

"This was a gift, for old time's sake. I hope you take this and use it to clean yourself up. Don't attempt to contact me again. I have friends in the DA's office and you don't want their attention. For God's sake I hope you can turn your life around but until you do, this will end it".

Hector turned away with a heavy heart for the boy he once knew and loved. He thought he had seen a flicker of embarrassment on Carlos's face at the end but he couldn't be sure. Maybe he just wanted to see it.

The last stop the couple made was to Sybil's apartment to say a private goodbye. She was nearing retirement age and still in good health. After a long career of helping others she now wanted to do something for herself. With Clarisse married to a fine man she felt her life was complete. She knew the story of her dad and Packo would be remembered. During the last Memorial Day Concert televised on PBS, her poignant testimony was read aloud on the broadcast by a Hollywood actress that Sybil did not know. It was an emotional meeting between the newlyweds and Sybil. They all talked about the strange destiny that had joined their lives together. They also reflected on the bright future awaiting them. Just as the newlyweds were turning to leave, Hector said.

"You have done so much for Clarisse and I that we could never repay your kindness and support. You saved Clarisse and that saved me. I know you would like to retire soon so hopefully this will help".

He handed a large grocery bag to Sybil. Her eyes welled with tears as she examined its contents.

"Where did you get all this money? I can't accept this. You two should use it to buy a house".

Hector reassured her the money was from an old savings account he had opened years ago and would not be missed. The source of the cash had been an unbelievably hot streak of poker winnings from his old Navy buddies during his active duty. These men lived in frequent danger and high stakes gambling was just part of their lifestyle. She could put it to better use then they could. Sybil was incredulous but remained trusting to the end.

"I don't know what to say"

"Say nothing just always be here for us".

The three shared a lingering embrace.

In the car, Clarisse asked Hector why he had changed his mind about holding on to the treasure until he could locate his cousin. Hector explained:

"My cousin showed up to our wedding yesterday. You didn't see him but he took me aside at the reception. He was not the same as he once was. Instead of coming to share our joy and meet you, he came asking for money. The Carlos I knew is dead. I'm afraid any money I gave him would go to a bad end but I couldn't send him away with nothing. I gave Carlos $500. He seemed satisfied. The rest I gave to Sybil. You always said we should give the money away to help improve people's lives. I think that is just what we did. Sybil will see to it".

Arturo Molina's treasure had at long last found its way to his estranged daughter. Through many turbulent years this outcome was preordained by an irresistible force of astonishing coincidence. Artie's wanderings, Packo's fruitless quest, Sybil's selfless service, Clarisse's rehabilitation, and Hector's commitment were all blended in the crucible of circumstance. The catalyst needed to trigger the chain reaction was found in the dark passages of Michigan Central Station.

Whistle Stop 29

EPILOGUE PART 2 2018

The 1967 Riot

Sybil Molina poured a second cup of coffee. One of her great pleasures in retirement was to relax on a Sunday morning after church and enjoy a leisurely read of the Free Press. This routine was especially pleasurable in the springtime. Today's weather was perfect, sunny skies and a refreshing breeze. The brilliant assortment of potted flowers made her deck overlooking her meticulously tended garden a haven of peace and reflection. In this sanctuary she would write letters, telephone friends and pray. The news this spring was all good. She had received a long letter from Clarisse and Hector and they were eagerly awaiting the arrival of their second child. Clarisse had found a job with the network affiliate in Chicago and Sybil had visited them in their beautiful home in Evanston on several occasions. Hector had found a job with a law firm downtown and was on a five year track to make partner. The money that Hector had gifted her had gone towards the purchase of a small home in Corktown just two blocks removed from both Tigers Stadium and Michigan Central Station. Coincidentally, her residence was barely a quarter of a mile from the neighborhood where the Keillor's and the Clancy's, the notorious boot-leggers, had been neighbors in the years before the war. Across the street on the same block stood the former home of Tiger's Hall of Famer Shorty Waverly and his wife Evelyn, where they had raised their family. The latest generations of these historic clans continue to live in the area to this day.

Sybil enjoyed the blessing of good health and indulged her love of travel. She had fulfilled a lifetime ambition by traveling to Europe on a splurge vacation with Hector and Clarisse the summer before their first child was born. Now she was considering a trip to Spain in the autumn. In many ways Sybil felt her life was complete.

Sybil found herself thinking frequently of her father and the unhappy circumstances of his life. That reflection did cause her some lingering unhappiness. Certainly a decorated war hero deserved more than the obscurity of a neglected burial plot in a forgotten corner of the cemetery. She visited his grave frequently and made sure it was always decorated with seasonal flowers and small American flags. She did the same for the headstone of Packo, whom she believed was her Dad's one companion and benefactor in his misery. It troubled her that she knew so little about the two men but over time her imagination filled in the blanks of her memories.

This particular morning while browsing the obituaries she noticed a name that caught her eye. The article reported that Colonel Jackson Holloway veteran of Vietnam and Desert Storm had died in the VA hospital here in Detroit. He had been a resident of the city for many years. The article included his biography and the names of his family members. His grandfather George, father Clem, and mother Althea were predeceased but he had a surviving cousin Julius who was currently serving as a Congressman for Michigan's 15th district. The name George Holloway seemed familiar but she could not immediately place it. Suddenly a faint recognition seized her. She raced to recover the box in her bedroom that contained her dad's medals and the documents she had preserved all these years. She quickly found the document she sought, a single sheet of note book paper now yellowed with age. Faded but still legible in neat cursive, was the name George Holloway and a local address and phone number. She remembered how, many years ago, she first discovered this cryptic clue and been completely baffled by its meaning. Now the same name appeared in an obituary as the grandfather of a Vietnam veteran who was about the same age as her Dad and who may well have served at the same time. She sat down on the edge of the bed stunned by the possible implications. Had George Holloway and Arturo Molina been acquainted? The only way she could unravel this mystery was to consult the name of the only living person mentioned in the obituary.

Congressman Julius Holloway had an office in Saginaw that was listed in the Detroit phone book. She called the number and to her amazement a voice answered saying "Julius Holloway, speaking." Sybil blurted out her story trying her best to remain coherent. She had seen Colonel Holloway's obituary and noticed the name of his grandfather George. She had reason to believe George had known her deceased father. Sybil mistook the silence on the other end of the line to be confusion or disinterest. It was neither. What was going through Julius's mind had stunned him to speechlessness. When he finally spoke it was recalling the events from many years ago.

"It is amazing you caught me here. I am leaving in two hours to accompany my cousin's body to his burial in Mississippi. I just dropped by to answer a few calls before I left town. Yes, I know about your father. He had saved the life of my cousin Jackson in Vietnam. Jackson attended a party in Detroit in 1968, the night the riot started because he believed your Dad would be there. Jackson was arrested in the riot. We were trying to find your Dad to be a defense witness at his trial. I went to your mother's apartment to see if she could help us. You were just a little girl at the time. Your mother said she did not know her husband's whereabouts but I left her the name and address for George, Jackson's grandfather for her to contact if she received any news about your Dad. We never heard from her after that".

Julius expressed a desire to accompany her to the cemetery to visit the grave of the hero that saved this cousin's life. Julius was certain that Jackson would want that. After all the time he had spent in life trying to locate his comrade it was extraordinary it would be Julius to find him at last. It was arranged that they would make the pilgrimage over the Memorial Day holiday. That was fitting.

The two continued their conversation for nearly a half hour, Sybil craving any details or memories that Julius could share. The information was to Sybil, like a great treasure lost for many years and forgotten by all. The fact she was talking with a man, who in life, knew her Dad's story, if not his person, was intensely moving. This man had spoken to her mother when she was just a little girl. Sybil's knowledge of her deceased father and his tragic history had just grown dramatically. It was the only first-hand account of his memory in her possession and she exalted over it. She now knew that her Dad's unhappy life had left expanding ripples in the great pool of human affairs that extended to today. All the lives Jackson Holloway had influenced for good after Vietnam owed a debt of gratitude to Arturo Molina's heroism many years before. Sybil understood, at last, that her father's life had not been solitary or purposeless. She now knew that all humans are connected in a mysterious web of destiny. Artie's story would go on. She had found her Dad at last,

Whistle Stop 30

JANUARY 5, 1988

The Last Ghost

The weather in Detroit was frigid even for early January. Lows were expected to dip below zero in the city with even more brutal cold gripping the suburbs. Such conditions in Detroit this time of year were predictable but always unwelcome. Mostly the population went about their daily business, enduring the misery and simply waited for spring. People tried to take comfort from the gradual lengthening of daylight at supper time signaling the inexorable progress toward warmer weather. But this encouragement was barely noticeable so early in the New Year.

There was much happening in the world that formed a towering background overshadowing local events. The Big Three automakers had come to grips with surging import sales, sparking aggressive incentives that would stimulate the domestic industry throughout 1988. The Challenger disaster was receding in the nation's memory and manned flights on the space shuttle were scheduled to resume. The costly and ultimately futile Soviet invasion of Afghanistan was approaching a decade of stalemate. The brutal Iran-Iraq war raged on with over a million killed and a brokered peace still months away. Most Americans did not understand either of these conflicts, but both would nudge the nation inexorably in the general direction of the World Trade Center attacks of September 11, more than a decade later. The last year of the Reagan administration produced continuing controversy over the Iran-Contra scandal but the administration would survive when President Reagan took responsibility for the affair. As expected the hopeful progress in nuclear arms control begun in the Reykjavik summit of 1986 was being critically re-evaluated. Journalists questioned whether Gorbachev could be trusted, a perennial debate over diplomacy with the Soviets since the end of WWII. Most significantly, as elections approached, the media focused the nation's attention on all things political. Who would survive the grueling campaign to become the next President?

Lost in this deluge of national concerns was an event of sweeping local consequence. The last Amtrak passenger train left Michigan Central Station at 12:05 PM on January 5, 1988 bound for Chicago. Later that evening the final arrival from Chicago would officially close the station after 75 years.

On hand that morning, Walter Steziak was the last ticket agent and the only person working the ticket counter. He was 65 years old, and had worked 30 years at the station. He was ready for retirement and had no fear of economic hardship. Mostly he felt sentimental; remembering all the famous persons he had seen over the years. It was a long list of the notable and notorious but infinitely more numbers were the anonymous multitudes. These hoards descended on the terminal daily seeking transport to a thousand destinations. Their tidal movement was the backdrop for Walters working life. The one ingredient missing from his daily routine was solitude. He sensed intuitively he would never adapt to that. Today, he decided to celebrate this occasion providing a large assortment of boxed Krispy Kreme doughnuts and coffee. He intended to offer passengers and other terminal employees a fond farewell to a time gone by. It was not long before Steziak concluded he had overdone his generosity as the morning waned with so few people passing through. There were sure to be leftover doughnuts.

Caleb "Corky" Conway was a janitor whose task of keeping the mostly empty terminal clean and tidy required less effort as closing day approached. He was only 30 years old with a wife and two toddlers to provide for. His imminent unemployment both frightened and depressed him. He was a contract employee, not a union member, so he had no back-stop to tide him over to a new job. Hopefully, he would land on his feet in some nearby downtown location. In the meantime he eyed the surplus of doughnuts at the ticket counter planning to take them home for dinner because his kids loved the delicious treats. Not a healthy meal but one that could fill a hungry belly.

In all there were some 45 staff people working that morning. In the terminal a small security detail had little trouble patrolling nearly deserted hallways. Most of the maintenance workers were already gone. On board the train was the usual contingent of engineers, conductors, and porters required by law to ensure safety. All would have the trajectory of their careers detoured this day by the stations closing. Some would benefit by these events going to better situations while others would be tragically set back and never recover.

The trip manifest included 75 passengers roughly half of the capacity of the train. Long abandoned by business travelers for the speed of air travel, railroad ridership was now the domain of occasional recreational travelers, students, working class commuters, and fearful flyers. Most of those on board were only vaguely aware they were characters on an historic journey. Most did not attach any great sentimentality to the trip. A few had made a mental note that their future travel plans would have to change. A very few were on board to celebrate the moment by completing the round trip between the two Great Lakes metropolises in a single day. There was one reporter from the Free Press on board intending to write a nostalgic piece for the Sunday paper about the end of an era.

The lights went out symbolically that evening in the station. Though empty, the building still maintained some usefulness. It would be years before it was completely surrendered to abandonment. Freight would still move along the tracks in its rail yard for some time. The cavernous inner spaces would provide storage until the buildings deterioration could no longer shut out the elements or intruders. The station would not completely decompose overnight but gradually. With every storm that buffeted the property, every destructive winter assault, every broken pipe or window, every maintenance task left undone, every municipal budget slashed, every widening crack in the masonry, all aggravated by the silent violence of time; the station declined into feral wreckage. For 30 years its deterioration would remain unimpeded.

There is circularity in history. All beginnings prefigure endings. Endings in turn become new beginnings. Could the lessons of history accumulated in Michigan Central Station be guiding us towards a brighter future for Detroit and the world? Can it be that the ghosts of Michigan Central are still whispering their pleas of remembrance to a generation finally listening?

Ingram Content Group UK Ltd.
Milton Keynes UK
UKHW011058310323
419467UK00001B/23

9 781958 729441